Conversation with Christ

*Dedicated to the First Friends Meeting (Whitewater Monthly Meeting)
of Richmond, Indiana, in whose Christian fellowship
these conversations took form.*

Acknowledgements

I thank Stephanie Ford, who shared some of these conversations
with her spiritual formation classes at the Earlham School of
Religion. She and her students offered helpful feedback. I am also
grateful to Barbara Mays for her friendly guidance as editor and
to Chel Avery for seeing the book through to production.

— *Douglas Gwyn*

Conversation *with* Christ

Quaker Meditations on the Gospel of John

Douglas Gwyn

QUAKERPRESS

PHILADELPHIA, PA

Copyright © 2011 QuakerPress of Friends General Conference
All rights reserved
1216 Arch Street 2B
Philadelphia, PA 19107

Printed in the United States of America.

Composition and design by David Botwinik.

ISBN 978-1-888305-92-0 (paperback)
    978-1-888305-91-3 (electronic version)

Library of Congress Cataloging-in-Publication Data
Gwyn, Douglas, 1948-
 Conversation with Christ : Quaker meditations on the Gospel of John / Douglas Gwyn.
    p. cm.
 ISBN 978-1-888305-92-0 (pbk.) -- ISBN 978-1-888305-91-3 (ebook) 1. Bible. N.T. John--
Meditations. 2. Society of Friends--Prayers and devotions. I. Title.
 BS2615.54.G99 2011
 226.5'06--dc22

                    2011010719

To order more copies of this publication or other Quaker titles call
1-800-966-4556 or see the online catalogue at www.quakerbooks.org

Contents

Introduction

This book is about growing in conversation with the living Christ. It explores thirteen conversations portrayed in the Gospel of John between Jesus and various individuals and groups. Those conversations may serve as templates for our own conversations with Christ. Through *conversation with* Christ, our *conversion to* Christ advances. That is, the conversations modeled in the Gospel of John suggest ways Christ may transform our lives. As we "listen in" on these conversations and reflect upon them in terms of our own experience, we may better recognize Christ present and active in our lives. We may further our own conversation with Christ.

The Gospel of John contrasts sharply with the other three gospels of the New Testament. The other gospels collect the sayings of Jesus. John offers extended conversations, dialogues. The other gospels remain engaged with concrete details and events in the ministry of Jesus. John's gospel takes events as the point of departure for conversation. When we read them carefully and reflectively, these conversations may move us to a place of stillness and peace. That is, *the conversations themselves* may take us toward the spiritual realm Jesus repeatedly witnesses. The Gospel of John is more than a report of the life of Jesus. It is a guide for readers and hearers to enter into that life, to move with Christ into the eternal reality Christ opens for all. John's conversations with Christ serve as portals into God's realm.

Following the work of C. K. Barrett, Paul Anderson [1997, pp. 60–67] emphasizes the dialogical quality of the Fourth Gospel. Not only do Jesus' teachings play out as conversations; we also see themes developed dialectically. Faith, for example, unfolds as a subtle interplay between seeing and not seeing, working and not working. Conversation is not only the verbal interaction of persons. Thought itself is essentially unspoken dialogue. As Socrates suggests in Plato's *Theatetus*, thought is "the conversation which the soul holds with herself." In terms of a

Christian perspective, conversations in the Gospel of John guide us into our interior conversation with Christ.

This book's approach to the Gospel of John draws on the historic Quaker approach to reading Scripture, although it is not be limited to Quakers. Traditionally, Friends (Quakers) have sought to know the truth of any biblical text in terms of their own experience (both past life experience and the present reading experience). That approach cuts through modern debates between literalist and historical-critical readings of the Bible. In mid-seventeenth-century England, George Fox (1624–91), the central figure in the early Quaker movement, realized that even the most strenuous affirmations (or denials) of matters witnessed in Scripture are mere human opinion.

> So I saw it was the fallen man that was got up into the Scriptures and was finding fault with . . . the backsliding Jews . . . that they were inwardly ravening wolves, that had got the sheep's clothing . . . etc. But when these, who were so much taken up with finding fault in others, and thought themselves clear from these things, came to look into themselves, and with the light of Christ thoroughly to search themselves, they might see enough of this in themselves; and then the cry could not be, it is he, or they, as before, but I and we are found in these conditions.
>
> I saw also how people read the scriptures without a right sense of them and without duly applying them to their own states. . . . They could not know the spiritual meaning of Moses', the prophets', and John's words, nor see their path and travels, much less see through them to the end of them into the kingdom unless they had the Spirit and light of Jesus; nor could they know the words of Christ and his apostles without his Spirit. But as man comes through by the Spirit and power of God to Christ . . . and is led by the Holy Ghost to the truth and substance of the scriptures, sitting down in him who is the author and end of them, then they are read and understood with profit and great delight [Fox (1952), pp. 30–32].

I would by no means deny the value of biblical scholarship or modern, critical methods of interpretation. I have learned much through such methods. But I affirm Fox's insight, that the truth-value of Scripture for the Christian reader is found in the encounter with Christ that is uniquely occasioned by a given passage at a given moment.

In the case of the Gospel of John, many centuries of scholarship have produced many layers of interpretation. There is much to explore in John's unique synthesis of Hebrew-Jewish and Greek thought, or his use of metaphor and irony, for example. Indeed, when we speak of "John" as the author, it is better to think of a whole community of preachers, prophets, writers and editors, spanning decades of development behind the text as we have it. The disciple John, presumably the "beloved disciple" in the Gospel, was probably only the central, originating figure in a complex history of the text's development. Memories from the life of Jesus were gradually elaborated by early Christian preaching and further developed into a literary whole. Participants in that process would not have imagined themselves "making up" material. Rather, they were continuing the revelation of the historical Jesus through the spiritual guidance of the risen Christ, the Spirit of Truth.

My method of interpreting the conversations in the Gospel of John mirrors process that produced them. Each chapter offers an interpretation of one of the conversations in the Gospel of John. The texts of the conversations are reproduced from the New Revised Standard Version of the Bible (1989). My exegesis has been informed by some of the best modern New Testament scholarship (see Works Cited at the end of this book for references to works chiefly used). But these chapters also share the fruit of my own years of study, meditation, teaching and preaching on the Gospel of John. Hopefully, these interpretations help the reader enter more fully into each of the conversations. At the end of each chapter, the reader is invited into a "guided conversation" which takes motifs from that particular passage in John as points of direct engagement with Christ. There, the reader's own conversation with Christ can unfold. This is one way to, as George Fox suggests, look into oneself, allow the light of Christ to search oneself, and be led by the Holy Spirit into the truth and substance of the Scriptures.

Through that process, Fox writes, one begins "to sit down in him who is the author and end" of Scripture. His language echoes Ephesians 2:6, which witnesses that God has "raised us up with [Christ] and seated us with him in the heavenly places in Christ Jesus." That higher plane of vision is the goal of each conversation in the Gospel of John. Jesus works with the incomprehension and mistaken assumptions of each individual and group, seeking to help them find the eternal dimension in their lives. For example, we will witness the well-intentioned bumbling of Nicodemus in John 3. He is described as a teacher of Israel, yet he seems clueless to the real meaning of Jesus' words. But (remembering Fox's warning) rather than feel superior to poor Nicodemus, we should recognize that we are just as obtuse in our own circumstances.

We too need to be taken up to that higher plane of vision. In the early centuries of the Church, theologians called this mystical sense the *anagogical* level of reading Scripture. The Greek *anagoge* means "leading or driving upwards." It is an ascending movement, not only lifting the *story* beyond its historical circumstances, but lifting *us* beyond our circumstances as well to meet Christ on another level. That level of reading is also called the *apocalyptic*, because it is a "removing of the veil" (the literal meaning of the Greek *apokalypsis*) of mundane appearances to reveal their hidden, eternal dimension. That revelatory moment, that ascending pattern, is built into the conversations John narrates in his gospel. The aim of the following chapters is to follow that movement into our own conversation with Christ.

Each chapter also includes reflections from the Quaker tradition. We will hear historic Quaker witness to the spiritual realities that arise in these conversations. Most examples will come from the first generation of Friends. Friends first appeared at a high water mark of biblical literacy in England. Their use of Scripture is remarkable. Their writings move consistently to the anagogical/apocalyptic meaning of the text, as they have found it through their own experience. Their witness offers a helpful bridge between our reading of John and the guided conversations.

My approach to these guided conversations is partly indebted to the "focusing" method developed by Eugene Gendlin (1982). Gendlin's framework is secular psychology, but his method readily lends itself to a spiritual, religious framework. Following Gendlin's approach, these conversations often invite the reader into what might be called a "negative moment." One may be asked to look at a dilemma or obstacle in life. The meditation invites the reader to *be still* at that sticking point, to see clearly and not run from it. As the reader spends a quiet moment in that negative space, she or he may find an opening into spiritual depth in Christ. Standing still and observing one's own life, one will likely find fear or frustration begin to ease. One senses a shift, an opening into true peace and communion in Christ.

The guided conversations offer the opportunity to know Christ here and now in the ways John's gospel describes: the light of the world, living water, the bread of life, the good shepherd, the gate, the vine, etc. These exercises may help the reader discover more acutely the reality of Christ's presence in his or her life. They may also stimulate one's prayer life generally and generate new insights, in whatever situations life presents.

The guided conversations invite readers to move to a deeper, bodily sense of a life situation. Paradoxically, by going "lower" into the body, we are led to a "higher" order of awareness, where Christ can more directly teach us. This should not be surprising, since Christ is "the word made flesh" (John 1:14). Our bodies, so often ignored, neglected, even abused by our willful hearts and hyperactive minds, are the privileged site of Christ's abiding presence and guidance.

The approach of these meditations is also indebted to the work of Rex Ambler (2001, 2002), a British Friend who has connected Gendlin's "focusing" method with the spiritual counsel found in George Fox's writings. Fox's spiritual guidance helped catalyze the early Quaker movement, but is largely unknown today, even among Friends. One purpose of this book is to reconnect Fox's spiritual practice with Scripture, which was clearly his framework of understanding. Although Fox used the Bible extensively, from Genesis to Revelation, the Gospel of John probably best defines his approach to life in Christ.

Readers may find the guided conversations more useful heard rather than read. Electronic versions are available through QuakerBooks of Friends General Conference (www.quakerbooks.org). These guided conversations may bring up difficult feelings, so a reader may wish to opt out if the experience becomes too troubling. Returning to the exercise another day may prove more helpful. In addition, a reader may wish to keep a personal journal of these experiences and insights or speak to a friend or spiritual director. Some readers may wish to form a group, where individuals may share their experiences and insights with the book and its guided conversations. Such extra steps may help in gaining more from the exercise.

I can attest that the writing of these chapters and the development of these meditations has been a rich experience and an advancement of my own Christian growth. May readers gain similar benefit from this book.

John 1:1–18: In the beginning was the Word, and the Word was with God, and the Word was God. He was in the beginning with God. All things came into being through him, and without him not one thing came into being. What has come into being in him was life, and the life was the light of all people. The light shines in the darkness, and the darkness did not overcome it.

There was a man sent from God, whose name was John. He came as a witness to testify to the light, so that all might believe through him. He himself was not the light, but he came to testify to the light. The true light, which enlightens everyone, was coming into the world.

He was in the world, and the world came into being through him; yet the world did not know him. He came to that which was his own, and his own people did not accept him. But to all who received him, who believed in his name, he gave power to become children of God, who were born, not of blood or of the will of the flesh or of the will of man, but of God.

And the Word became flesh and lived among us, and we have seen his glory, the glory as of a father's only son, full of grace and truth. (John testified to him and cried out, "This is he of whom I said, 'He who comes after me ranks ahead of me because he was before me.'") From his fullness we have all received, grace upon grace, The law indeed was given through Moses; grace and truth came through Jesus Christ. No one has ever seen God. It is God the only Son, who is close to the Father's heart, who has made him known.

Before we enter into these conversations, it may be useful briefly to consider the sublime Prologue to the Gospel of John. Probably based upon a Christ hymn of John's community, the Prologue functions as an overture to several major themes of the Gospel. Indeed, we might think of it as an *overture to conversation*. The Prologue expresses in *principle* what the ensuing chapters dramatize in *practice*. As the Word incarnate, Jesus engages the world in a revealing conversation, one that goes to the heart of the truth. But again and again, as we shall see, even his own people do not understand. Or as the King James Version renders verse 5, our darkness does not *comprehend* the light. But as we simply *receive* Christ, we begin to believe. In so doing, we receive the power to become children of God. And "from his fullness we have all received, grace upon grace" (verse 16).

There is both majesty and subtlety to John's Prologue. It uniquely intertwines Greek and Hebrew understandings of the Word. It is a poetic distillation of the meaning of the gospel, in the fullest cosmic terms. But just as the Word becomes flesh by actually dwelling among us, by engaging in concrete conversation with us, so the poetry of the Prologue comes to life through the drama of the ensuing chapters. And that drama moves into the framework of our own stories as we engage the living Christ in our own conversation.

Disciples
John 1:35–51

All four New Testament gospels describe the beginning of Jesus' ministry in connection with John the Baptist. Yet each portrays only a brief encounter between Jesus and John. We easily gain the impression that Jesus simply met the Baptist one day at the Jordan River, was baptized and hailed as the Messiah, and then left to begin his ministry. But John's gospel hints at something more.

Jesus may have been with the Baptist for a period of time before the latter proclaimed him the Son of God. Twice John the Baptist exclaims, "I myself did not know him" (1:31a, 33a), implying perhaps that it took time to discern Jesus as the Messiah, the one whose way he was preparing. However, if Jesus did spend time with John, it appears that he was probably not the latter's disciple. The Fourth Gospel doesn't actually say that John baptized Jesus. And later (4:1–2), it mentions that Jesus himself didn't baptize anyone, although his disciples did. We know from the present story that at least two of Jesus' disciples were former disciples of John. So perhaps *they* continued John's practice of water baptism, and Jesus evidently allowed it.

My point in these observations is to suggest that the Baptist not only *prepared the way* for Jesus through his ministry in the wilderness. He may have *prepared Jesus* in some ways as well. And for his part, Jesus looked back on John as "a burning and shining lamp" (5:35). It is important to maintain this human perspective on Jesus, particularly since the Fourth Gospel portrays him in such exalted terms.

1:35–42: The next day John again was standing with two of his disciples, and as he watched Jesus walk by, he exclaimed, "Look, here is the Lamb of God!" The two disciples heard him say this, and they followed Jesus. When Jesus turned and saw them following, he said to them, "What are you looking for?" They said to him, "Rabbi" (which translated means Teacher), "where are you staying?" He said to them,

"Come and see." They came and saw where he was staying, and they remained with him that day. It was about four o'clock in the afternoon. One of the two who heard John speak and followed him was Andrew, Simon Peter's brother. He first found his brother Simon and said to him, "We have found the Messiah" (which is translated Anointed). He brought Simon to Jesus, who looked at him and said, "You are Simon son of John. You are to be called Cephas (which is translated Peter).

In John 1:29, John the Baptist declares Jesus "the Lamb of God who takes away the sin of the world," for he has seen the Spirit descend like a dove upon Jesus. He recognizes it as a sign from God. Our passage takes up the next day, when John looks at Jesus and again declares him to be the Lamb of God. The two disciples of John standing by leave to follow Jesus. We are told that one of them was Andrew, brother of Simon Peter. The other is left unnamed. Many have thought this to be the "beloved disciple," mentioned several times in the Fourth Gospel and credited to be the Gospel's author, or primary source. And generally, the beloved disciple has been identified with the disciple John. If that is the case, then the principle source of the Fourth Gospel has inserted himself almost unnoticed into the story.

Jesus turns and notices the two men following him. He asks them the question that addresses all who would follow him: "What are you looking for?" All seeking begins with some sense of aim, no matter how vague or misdirected. The disciples ask, "Rabbi, where are you staying?" Although they have heard their master proclaim this man the Lamb of God, they begin cautiously, addressing him merely as "Rabbi" and asking where he is staying. There is another level to their question, however. A recurring theological motif in the Gospel of John is the origins and abiding place of Jesus. For example, the opponents of Jesus admit, "we do not know where he comes from" (9:29). They do not recognize his heavenly origins and destiny with the Father. So the two disciples of John, typical of many in the Gospel who talk to Jesus, do not grasp the full implications even of their own questions (let alone the answers they receive). But Jesus honors their cautious sincerity. He accepts their terms of address and responds to their question with an open-ended, "Come and see." He gently invites these avid young men to join him on an unfolding journey, a *dialogue of discovery*. Eventually, they will understand where this Jesus truly abides. But the journey begins with mundane lodgings.

We are not told how long they stay with Jesus, but one of them, Andrew, becomes convinced Jesus is much more than a teacher. He finds his brother, Simon, and blurts out, "We have found the Messiah." When Jesus meets Simon, he sees into him and discerns his true character. "You are Simon son of John. You are to be called Cephas (which is translated Peter)." Jesus recognizes a rock-like solidity in Simon. This is ironic, of course, given that all four gospels portray Peter as impetuous and volatile. At the end, after promising to defend Jesus to the death, Peter denies him three times. But from the very beginning, looking into Simon, Jesus sees beyond all that. More than that, in *naming* Simon Cephas, Jesus *calls* him to *become* something. That rock-solid quality will not emerge in Peter until later, when the movement will urgently require a central, steadfast leader. But in this initial moment, by renaming Simon Cephas/Peter, Jesus sets him upon a new course, toward a new horizon. To the extent that Simon Peter believes Jesus, he has begun the journey.

> **1:43-51:** The next day Jesus decided to go to Galilee. He found Philip and said to him, "Follow me." Now Philip was from Bethsaida, the city of Andrew and Peter. Philip found Nathaniel and said to him, "We have found him about whom Moses in the law and also the prophets wrote, Jesus son of Joseph from Nazareth." Nathaniel said to him, "Can anything good come out of Nazareth?" Philip said to him, "Come and see." When Jesus saw Nathaniel coming toward him, he said of him, "here is truly an Israelite in whom there is no deceit!" Nathaniel asked him, "Where did you get to know me?" Jesus answered, "I saw you under the fig tree before Philip called you." Nathaniel replied, "Rabbi, you are the Son of God! You are the King of Israel!" Jesus answered, "Do you believe because I told you that I saw you under the fig tree? You will see greater things than these." And he said to him, "Very truly, I tell you, you will see heaven opened and the angels of God ascending and descending upon the Son of Man."

Now Jesus abruptly decides to go to Galilee. Before leaving, Jesus finds Philip and tells him, "Follow me." As a Rabbi, Jesus was a teacher in the ancient mode of instruction, which was as much a matter of *mentoring* and *modeling* as didactic instruction. So Jesus invites Philip into not only a *conversation* of faith but a *conversion* to himself. Philip understands that he is not only to follow Jesus' ideas, but to follow his movements as well, to form his own life in the pattern Jesus demonstrates. Evidently, he is a quick learner. Soon after Jesus finds him, he follows that example and finds Nathaniel. Philip tells Nathaniel, "We have found him about whom Moses in the law and also the prophets wrote, Jesus son of Joseph from Nazareth."

Notice how, in a compressed literary fashion, John combines the various messianic figures the Jewish people are expecting, and which these disciples find confirmed in Jesus. We have now heard him called Son of God, Lamb of God, Messiah, and the Prophet. (This last was prophesied by Moses in Deuteronomy 18:15: "The Lord your God will raise up for you a prophet like me from among your own people".) But apparently none of these titles are declared to his face. We have heard them address Jesus only as "Rabbi." Still, they are sudden evangelists, quick to speak to others about Jesus in the most exalted terms.

Nathaniel introduces astringent, critical reservation (even sarcasm) to this expansive, credulous mood. He retorts, "Can anything good come from Nazareth?" But Philip employs Jesus' own pedagogy with Nathaniel. He counters, "Come and see." Apparently, Nathaniel is curious enough to go and meet Jesus himself. But John tells the story ambiguously here. It is possible that Jesus is only a few yards away, able to observe, even hear the conversation between Philip and Nathaniel. When Nathaniel approaches him, Jesus hails him, "Here is truly an Israelite in whom there is no deceit!" Perhaps Jesus has simply overheard Nathaniel's tart rejoinder and appreciates his forthrightness. (After all, Jesus knows Nazareth very well!) Nathaniel is caught off guard and responds cautiously, "Where did you get to know me?" "I saw you under the fig tree before Philip called you," Jesus explains. Again, if Jesus was only a few yards away, there is no clairvoyance involved here. We cannot know for sure. In any case, Nathaniel clearly assumes Jesus' knowledge of him to be miraculous and is the first to confess Jesus to his face: "Rabbi you are the Son of God! You are the King of Israel!" (The messianic titles for Jesus are now almost complete.) Nathaniel has suddenly turned from cynical doubter into gushing enthusiast.

Jesus teasingly answers, "Do you believe because I saw you under the fig tree?" (Again, how far away was Jesus standing?) But he adds, "You will see greater things than these. . . . Very truly I tell you, you will see heaven opened and the angels of God ascending and descending upon the Son of Man." The messianic title Jesus claims for himself here is *Son of Man*. This title evokes the most paradoxical of messianic expectations. The four gospels record it as the title Jesus most often associated with himself. Moreover, he nearly always spoke of the Son of Man in the third person, as he does here. This usage opens a way into the paradox of the Gospel of John.

Son of Man

Son of Man has a range of meanings in the Hebrew tradition (for a provocative exploration, see Walter Wink's *The Human Being: Jesus and the Enigma of the Son of the Man*). It can mean simply a human being. In the Book of Ezekiel, the Lord addresses the prophet many times as "son of man" with no special status implied. The prophet Daniel envisions "one like a son of man coming with the clouds of heaven" (Dan. 7:13–14). But literally, the verse simply says that this figure looks like a human being, in contrast to the four beasts of preceding visions. Owing in part to Daniel's vision, Jewish expectation developed concerning a coming Son of Man whose arrival would mark the end-time, who would judge all the peoples of the world. Son of Man—or Human Being—is apparently the title Jesus found most resonant with his own identity and mission. It maintains a tension between human and divine overtones. The Son of Man might be as common and universal as a carpenter's son from Galilee *and* might be God's agent of salvation. In his Prologue, John witnesses that Jesus is the divine Word made flesh, who came into the world in human form (John 1:14). Yet the same Prologue affirms that the same light enlightens all people (John 1:9). So the title Son of Man expresses in a peculiarly Jewish idiom the paradoxical union of divine and human, unique and universal, identities in Jesus.

Jesus promises his new disciples that they shall see heaven opened, with the Son of Man stretching between heaven and earth, and angels ascending and descending upon him. It is a powerful image of Jesus as both human and divine, bridging heaven and earth, eternity and time, divine Spirit and human flesh. But there is a corresponding ambiguity regarding the angels. The Hebrew or Aramaic behind John's Greek may imply divine agents or simply "messengers." Are these "angels" heavenly beings? Or are they human messengers, even the disciples themselves? Like the three angels who visited Abraham by the oaks of Mamre (Gen. 18–20), it may be difficult to discern. Referring to the story of Abraham, the Letter to the Hebrews (13:2) warns, "Do not neglect to show hospitality to strangers, for by doing that some have entertained angels without knowing it." So the disciples are implicated in the same human-divine ambiguity that Jesus himself has embraced with the title Son of Man.

The promise Jesus makes here describes the path of discovery ahead of the disciples—and for anyone who enters into conversation with Christ. They are in awe of Jesus and have bestowed on him just about every messianic title they know. Nathaniel in particular has swung suddenly from skepticism to enthusiasm (possibly owing to a misunderstanding). In the next years, they will behold divine glory in a common man, even in his grisly public execution. As their vision of Jesus moves toward integration, they will find *themselves* enacting the same integration *in him*, bridging heaven and earth as messengers of the gospel. As they spread the message, they will impart to others the light and life they beheld in Jesus. Along the way, however, they will recognize something of that light in each person they encounter (again, see John 1:9). The Son of Man is uniquely embodied in Jesus of Nazareth, the Word made flesh. But the same Son of Man, the Human Being, is all of us.

It is worth noting a similar statement reported by Matthew, albeit in different terms. Near the end of his life, Jesus prophesies that false messiahs will come. People will claim to have found the Messiah here or there, in this individual here or that one there. Jesus warns his friends not to believe such claims. "For as lightning comes from the east and flashes as far as the west, so will be the coming of the Son of Man" (Matthew 24:27). The Son of Man will be revealed *everywhere*, coming through *everyone*.

So with these initial exchanges (from the simple "Come and see" to the vision of the Son of Man) Jesus calls his disciples. Like so many conversations in the Gospel of John, it begins with earthly, mundane questions ("Where are you staying?") and moves quickly into intimations of the sublime. Yet even the sublime will prove to be grounded in practical conversation, as the disciples learn their roles as messengers/angels of Christ. The unfolding conversation that reveals *who Jesus is* simultaneously defines *who we are in him*.

Reflections from the Quaker Tradition

The Quaker movement arose in England in the 1650s, at a time of political conflict and religious experimentation. The early Quaker message attracted a variety of men and women desperate to ground their lives in a direct experience of God. Many were called Seekers, because they had dropped out from all churches, to wait and watch for new apostles whom they expected would rebuild the Church upon the foundation of Christ's living presence. They had followed many different teachers and sampled various alternative forms of worship, and many felt bereft and bewildered. Sarah Blackborow, who joined the Quaker movement in London in the mid-1650s, published a tract to Seekers, *A Visit to the Spirit in Prison* (1658). There she addresses the seeking condition bluntly but compassionately:

> Wisdom hath uttered forth her voice to you, but the eye and ear which is abroad, waiting upon the sound of words without you, is that which keeps you from your Teacher within you; and this is the reason that in all your seeking you have found nothing; such as your seeking is, such is your finding. . . . Therefore . . . come out of the manie things; theres but one thing needful, keep to it . . . that into my Mother's house you all may come, and into the Chamber of her that conceived me, where you may embrace, and be embraced of my dearly beloved one, Love is his name, Love is his Nature, Love is his life [see Song of Solomon 3:1–4] [Garman, *et. al.*, 1996, pp. 52, 55].

Whatever spiritual truths Seekers had learned from various teachers, they had fallen short of the truth that comes only from the inward teacher. Similarly, the drama narrated in John, where Jesus begins an outward conversation with his disciples, must serve as a figure for the inward drama, where Christ draws us into an interior conversation. Sarah Blackborow here redirects Seekers into a different conversation than the one they've been pursuing. Her language beautifully blends feminine and masculine overtones. Like other early Quaker writers, she draws her imageries from the Hebrew and Christian Scriptures. But her witness also resonates with a variety of spiritual teachings today that emphasize that the inward journey involves an interplay of masculine and feminine archetypes within the human psyche. Blackborow witnesses to an inward Christ who is transgendered, but may speak to us variously with feminine or masculine overtones.

Blackborow's witness invites us to begin that inward dialogue with Christ. Another early Friend describes something of the journey that unfolds from there. Luke Cock was an uneducated butcher and a singer of some note living in Northeast Yorkshire, when he found the inward teacher. He became a Friend and eventually a Friends minister. Below is an excerpt from a sermon he preached at York in 1721. His rural Yorkshire speech and imagery are rough hewn. Yet his witness to his Guide speaks with the authority of experience:

> Necessity, Friends, outstrips the law: necessity has made many people go by the Weeping Cross.... I remember I was yonce travelling through Shrewsbury, and my Guide said to me: "I'll show thee the Weeping Cross." "Nay," said I, "thou need not; I have borne it a great while." Now this place he showed me was four lane ends.

There is a landmark crossroads east of Shrewsbury called the Weeping Cross. So in this first instance, Cock may be speaking of a human guide, who offered to show him a local site. But he will use it as an image for his journey with the inward Guide.

> I remember when I first met with my Guide. He led me into a very large and cross [place], where I was to speak the truth from my heart—and before I used to swear and lie too for gain. "Nay, then," said I to my Guide, "I mun leave Thee here: if Thou leads me up that lane, I can never follow: I'se be ruined of this butchering trade, if I mun't lie for a gain." Here I left my Guide, and was filled with sorrow, and went back to the Weeping Cross: and I said, if I could find my good Guide again, I'll follow Him, lead me whither He will. So here I found my Guide again, and began to follow Him up this lane and tell the truth from my heart. I had been nought but beggary and poverty before; and now I began to thrive at my trade, and got to the end of this lane, though with some difficulty.

Early Friends were noted (and notorious) for their plain and truthful speaking. They refused to lie, to swear oaths, to use flowery or flattering language, or to barter. In their refusal to haggle, Friends became pioneers of the one-price trading system in seventeenth-century England. They set a fair price for their goods and refused to bargain. The practice, begun as a matter of personal integrity in business, proved very popular with customers and contributed to the widespread success of

Quakers in business. So we hear Luke Cock witness to the first frightening "lane" where his Guide led him, as he adopted one-price trading. And we hear of the success he was surprised to discover.

> But now my Guide began to lead me up another lane, harder than the first, which was to bear my testimony in using the plain language. This was very hard; yet I said to my Guide, "Take my feeble pace, and I'll follow Thee as fast as I can. Don't outstretch me, I pray Thee." So by degrees I got there.

Quaker plainness of language often led to variety of awkward encounters. They were unable to use deferential language toward social superiors or to engage in verbal niceties. And they addressed all individuals using "thee" or "thou." "You" had been reserved in earlier English usage for plural addressees. By the seventeenth century, however, polite speech addressed an individual of higher social rank as "you." By returning to the earlier usage, Friends resisted another subtle form of social hierarchy. Such matters of daily interaction often turned early Friends into social pariahs. In court, when they would not remove their hat, swear an oath, or address the judge as "you," it could lead to more serious problems. So this was another "lane" Cock dreaded, but found he could walk with his Guide.

> But now I was led up the third lane: it was harder still, to bear my testimony against tithes—my wife not being convinced. I said to my Guide, "Nay, I doubt I never can follow up here: but don't leave me: take my pace, I pray thee, for I mun rest me." So I tarried here a great while, till my wife cried, "We'se all be ruined: what is thee ganging stark mad to follow t'silly Quakers?" Here I struggled and cried, and begged of my Guide to stay and take my pace: and presently my wife was convinced. "Well," says she, "now follow thy Guide, let come what will. The Lord hath done abundance for us: we will trust in Him." Nay, now, I thought, I'll to my Guide again, now go on, I'll follow Thee truly; so I got to the end of this lane cheerfully.

Even after their persecutions ended with the Act of Toleration in 1689, Friends continued to suffer fines and other legal actions for their continued refusal to pay tithes in support of the Church of England. Cock's wife was not "convinced of the Truth," as early Friends called those who joined in their way of faithfulness. Given the legal consequences of tithe resistance and the more consensual style of marriage among Friends, he was unable to follow his Guide down this "lane" for some years, apparently. But as she too was convinced, his wife found considerable boldness of faith, and they were able to proceed together.

> My Guide led me up another lane, more difficult than any of the former, which was to bear testimony to that Hand that had done all this for me. This was a hard one: I thought I must never have seen the end of it. I was eleven years all but one month in it. Here I began to go on my knees and to creep under the hedges, a trade I never forgot since, nor I hope never shall. I would fain think it is impossible for me to fall now, but let him that thinks he stands take heed lest he fall.

Here Cock witnesses to his calling to public ministry. The traditional form of ministry among Friends contains many challenges. One must maintain another form of livelihood, yet somehow arrange to go on occasional travels in ministry, which interrupt business and family life and strain finances. Moreover, one must travel and speak only by the guidance of the Spirit. This "lane" of the cross was the greatest challenge. The imagery of walking on his knees and crawling under hedges suggests the difficulty. He was tested and stretched by his Guide down all four "lanes," but also strengthened by each.

> I thought to have had a watering: but ye struggle so I cannot get you together. We mun have no watering tonight, I mun leave you every yan to his own Guide [sermon quoted in Britain Yearly Meeting, 1995, 20:22].

This final excerpt from Cock's sermon offers a hint of the Quaker understanding of baptism. Friends have traditionally understood baptism to be an inward and spiritual reality. For that reason, they do not practice outward, ritual baptism with water. It could mislead an individual into believing that the rite has accomplished the true, inward reality of baptism. Further, in traditional Quaker worship, a powerful message may "gather" the group into a sense of the Spirit's "covering," a sense of being submerged in the Spirit's baptizing power. Here, Cock disappointedly acknowledges his sense that his sermon has not produced a "watering" of the meeting. So in concluding, all he can do is leave each participant to his or her own inward Guide, to wait in silence upon the Lord's direct teaching.

As Luke Cock left his hearers at York in 1721 to their own Guide, this chapter closes with a meditation that may draw the reader to his or her own Guide.

Guided Conversation

The following offers an opportunity to contemplate a time when you were "called" in some particular way.

As with all the meditations in this book, it is important to take time to be quiet. Find a quiet place to sit for twenty to thirty minutes or more. Sit in a comfortable but upright position. Still your body for a few moments. Feel yourself breathing; perhaps notice the pulse somewhere in your body. As you come to a place of quiet, calm awareness say, "Here I am."

Now, think of a time you felt somehow called, nudged, led by an inner impulse you can identify with God, Spirit, Christ—a moment that seemed to say, "Follow me," or, "Come and see," or "Do this." Choose a time that you feel that you responded, that you followed, went and saw, acted. Take time to remember the circumstances. What was happening in your life at that time?

What did the calling or leading feel like? Try to locate that sense in your body. Does it locate in your chest, your stomach, your head or hands, or just all over? Take time to find that sense. Somewhere, your body will remember.

What word or words can you put to that sense? What captures that feeling for you? Don't go into an extended description. Just find a word or phrase. Your body will tell you when you have found the right words. After you feel you have found them, sit with them for a few moments.

Now ask, why was it that way? Don't go into a long explanation. Find something brief, just a few words that keep you connected with that sense in your body. If the words lead you away from that sense, let them go and ask again.

After you have settled on some words that fit the experience, stay there for a few moments. You may receive an insight into that experience, or something that helps you sense and follow other callings in the future. Most of all, try to stay grounded in the felt, bodily sense of the experience.

When the sense has faded and you cannot find it again, or when you feel ready to end the meditation, take some time in prayer, giving thanks for that experience, and for this present moment with Christ. Reaffirm your intention to be ready when the call comes again.

Learning to tune into the felt, bodily sense will help you more clearly identify and follow Christ's callings in the future. Remember, Christ is the Word made flesh in the person of Jesus of Nazareth—and in you. The Son of Man brings heaven and earth together. Spirit and flesh become one in our bodies. As we become more conscious in our bodies of Christ's presence and leading, we learn to abide with Christ more steadily.

Nicodemus

John 3:1–21

The conversation with Nicodemus takes place as Jesus' ministry has gained momentum and has caught the attention of religious leaders. Nicodemus appears to be a member of the ruling body of the people, a council composed of chief priests and leading Scribes and Pharisees. (This body also collaborated with the Roman authorities in keeping the local peace.) John portrays Nicodemus and Joseph of Arimathea as leaders sympathetic to Jesus (although they will prove unable to sway the council in Jesus' favor at his trial—see John 11:45–53; 18:1–24).

John portrays this conversation taking place at night. That detail may simply be historical: a leading Pharisee might not wish to be seen talking to a controversial prophet. Or it may be symbolic: Nicodemus is still "in the dark" about Jesus and his teaching (the theme of darkness will return at the end of this conversation).

3:1–10: Now there was a Pharisee named Nicodemus, a leader of the Jews. He came to Jesus by night and said to him, "Rabbi, we know that you are a teacher who has come from God; for no one can do these signs that you do apart from the presence of God." Jesus answered him, "Very truly, I tell you, no one can see the kingdom of God without being born from above." Nicodemus said to him, "How can anyone be born after having grown old? Can one enter a second time into the mother's womb and be born?" Jesus answered, "Very truly, I tell you, no one can enter the kingdom of God without being born of water and Spirit. What is born of the flesh is flesh, and what is born of the Spirit is spirit. Do not be astonished that I said to you, 'You must be born from above.' The wind blows where it chooses, and you hear to the sound of it, but you do not know where it comes from or where it goes. So it is with everyone who is born of the Spirit." Nicodemus said to him, "How can these things be?" Jesus answered him, "Are you a teacher of Israel and yet you do not understand these things?"

Nicodemus evidently approaches Jesus with respect and good intentions. He offers that Jesus must be sent from God; otherwise he could not perform such wondrous signs. Now so far, John has mentioned only two signs: turning water into wine at Cana and driving money changers from the temple in Jerusalem. If Nicodemus approves the second act, he is surely a reformer among the leaders. Nevertheless, Jesus wastes no time on his affirmation. Instead, he warns Nicodemus that he will neither see nor enter the kingdom of God unless he is born from above, by the Spirit.

Jesus implies that, even with good intentions, Nicodemus has only offered an *inference*, a mental deduction. That is: Jesus has done these remarkable things; therefore, he must be sent from God; he must have God's presence with him. But Jesus counters friendly approval with a stark challenge: *see* God's presence; *enter* God's realm. As a teacher of the Torah, Nicodemus teaches the history of Israel and applies the law, based upon certain casuistic principles of deduction. But Jesus calls him to an immediate experience of God's will through the power of the Spirit. Moreover, that shift in *knowing* the will of God requires nothing less than a shift in *being*, a rebirth by the Spirit. Nicodemus has come with good intentions, even accurate inferences. But Jesus answers, "You can't get here from there." John's gospel asserts several times this gulf between light and darkness, between good and evil, between spiritual and circumstantial ways of knowing. But in this conversation, Jesus states the case most acutely.

In the Gospel of John, individuals and groups routinely misperceive Jesus. They misunderstand the real intention of his words. But no one falls flatter than Nicodemus, this respected teacher. He blankly wonders (or jests?), how can one be born again in old age? How one can re-enter the mother's womb? It would be accurate to say that Jesus speaks metaphorically, while Nicodemus construes his words literally. But the answer to literalism is not simply reading John with more literary sophistication. The reality Jesus witnesses here is not "like" being born. It is a kind of rebirth! It shifts the very foundations of one's being. "Very truly [*Amen, Amen*], I tell you," Jesus begins. He calls Nicodemus to the realm of truth, beyond both literal and literary understandings of his words.

When Jesus speaks of "being born of water and Spirit," many Christians assume he refers to the rite of baptism. But the symbolic use of water in Christian baptism is simply a physical metaphor. As such, it falls short of the reality Jesus declares. Recall that John pointedly mentions that Jesus baptized no one. Here, Jesus mentions *water* and *Spirit* in parallel with flesh and Spirit. ("What is born of the flesh is flesh, and what is born of the Spirit is spirit.") So clearly, the water in question here is the amniotic water of the womb, released with the first birth. The release of the Spirit replaces the release of water at the second birth.

After declaring rebirth as a change in being, Jesus returns to the question of knowing that began the conversation. Using normal human reckoning, one remains mystified by the Spirit's movement—and equally confused by people who are moved by the Spirit. Nicodemus confirms Jesus' observation as he responds blankly (or impatiently?), "How can these things be?" Jesus chides, "And you're a teacher of Israel?"

> **3:11–16:** "Very truly, I tell you, we speak of what we know and testify to what we have seen; yet you do not receive our testimony. If I told you about earthly things and you do not believe, how can you believe if I tell you about heavenly things? No one has ascended into heaven except the one who descended from heaven, the Son of Man. And just as Moses lifted up the serpent in the wilderness, so must the Son of Man be lifted up, that whoever believes in him may have eternal life. For God so loved the world that he gave his only Son, that everyone who believes in him may not perish but may have eternal life."

Jesus continues: he and his followers teach what they see and know, "yet you [plural] do not receive our testimony." Jesus refers here not only to Nicodemus but to the other leaders of the people. Even a sympathetic listener doesn't *get* the message. It is lost in transmission, because it comes from another domain. It does not translate. Jesus has stated the case in the most elemental, even earthly terms. How will poor Nicodemus understand if Jesus really begins speaking the language of heaven?

Jesus next pursues the matter on different terms, more idiomatic to the contemporary Jewish faith. He adds that only the Son of Man communicates heaven and earth, reaches to both realms. (We heard that imagery at the end of the preceding conversation, after Jesus called his disciples.) Jesus suggests here that only the Son of Man can imbue Nicodemus (or anyone) with a sense of heavenly things. Jesus then offers a figure from the Torah, the realm of Nicodemus' expertise.

In the wilderness, when the people were bitten by poisonous snakes, Moses lifted up a bronze serpent on a pole. Those who looked to the bronze serpent were saved (see Num. 21:4–9). Similarly, the Son of Man must be lifted up before the people if they are to believe and live. Jesus uses a strange story from Israel's wilderness saga to speak of his coming death (being "lifted up" on the cross) and its saving effect for humanity.

Moses' strange cure is almost homeopathic. Viewing the image of a cursed serpent cancels the deadly effect of snake venom. Jesus uses that weird story to imply that the Son of Man *becomes* the curse of our human condition with its flaws, in order to *free* us from it. He *saves* us from our own darkness, *translates* our being and our minds into heaven's own idiom. Nothing less will accomplish that profound change in us. Again, conversation leads toward conversion, and conversion advances the conversation on new terms.

How does this impossible, astonishing translation come? Only the love of God could will and accomplish such a thing. This Son of Man, sharing—indeed, consummately *bearing*—our curse and the death it exacts, is in fact *God's only Son*. He is given "so that everyone who believes in him may not perish but may have eternal life." As we saw in the preceding conversation, the Son of Man, the Human Being, represents all of us. All of us need to see this Human Being, *our human being*, offered up to die, if we are to receive his spiritual, heavenly, eternal life. Sensing God's inviting love, we are able to risk such surrender.

> **3:17–21:** "Indeed, God did not send the Son into the world to condemn the world, but in order that the world might be saved through him. Those who believe in him are not condemned; but those who do not believe are condemned already, because they have not believed in the name of the only Son of God. And this is the judgment, that the light has come into the world, and people loved the darkness rather than the light because their deeds were evil. For all who do evil hate the light and do not come to the light, so that their deeds may not be exposed. But those who do what is true come to the light, so that it may be clearly seen that their deeds have been done in God."

The situation is hopeless: Nicodemus cannot by his best efforts even peek into the kingdom of God, much less enter it. And how will he believe in God's only Son, whose words are so opaque to him? Those who believe in the Son are not condemned. But those who do not believe are condemned already. Again, there seems to be an absolute, unbridgeable gulf between Jesus and Nicodemus. The verses that follow offer a resolution. Indeed, they return to the issues Jesus raised at the start of the conversation: flesh versus spirit, seeing the kingdom of God, being born again.

John 3:16 is a favorite among Christians (especially those attending sporting events, apparently). But the decisive statement in this conversation comes in verse 19. That is the secret to getting "from here to there." "And this is the judgment, that the light has come into the world." The Greek for "judgment" is *krisis*. It is the noun form of the verb translated "condemn" in verses 17 and 18. The difference between *judgment* and *condemnation* consists simply in how one responds to the crisis, the confrontation with the light of Christ. The moment of crisis, the confrontation with the light, is a moment of freedom. Humans respond to its revelation freely, coming to the light or fleeing from it. The outcome of that human response spells redemption or condemnation. Moreover, those who flee are "condemned already." This statement sounds to some Christians like an affirmation of divine predestination: i.e., the teaching that one is already saved or damned from before the beginning of time. But it is determined instead by John's *eschatology*, his sense that the end is already present.

Jesus draws here upon the Jewish expectation that the Son of Man will come in the last days to judge all humanity. "Judgment day," a final day of reckoning, is a centerpiece of both Jewish and Christian end-time expectation. It is the *apocalyptic* moment when God *exposes* all things—and all people—as they truly are. But Jesus, the Son of Man, declares the judgment to be a present reality. It has already begun. The light has come into the world. It's a painful revelation, to be sure: "people loved the darkness rather than light because their deeds were evil. For all who do evil hate the light and do not come to the light, so that their deeds may not be exposed."

We all err and sin. But our sin becomes *evil* only as we hide it from the light, as we live in denial of the truth about ourselves. Under the cover of willed darkness, our simple, even innocent mistakes may do real mischief in our lives, and in the world. We begin to rationalize and justify them, turning them into habits of mind and body. Then, it becomes more difficult to come to the light.

"But those who do what is true come to the light, so that it may be clearly seen that their deeds have been done in God." In the Bible, and particularly in John's gospel, "truth" is less a proposition to be believed than a faithful, consistent life that embodies God's love and God's Word in the world. As the incarnation of God's Word, Jesus is himself the truth (see Conversation 9). Those who act in truth easily come to the light, because it reveals and validates the truth of their actions.

The conversation ends here. It appears that we are still faced with an unbridgeable gulf, now stated in terms of those who do evil and lurk in darkness *versus* those who do the truth and come to the light. But this is *precisely* where Nicodemus (and all of us with him) are left, with the challenge to step into the light, whether our deeds are true or false, good or evil. The sublime love expressed in 3:16 is only a platitude if we do not step into the light, the judgment day Jesus proclaims in 3:19. *Believing* that God's only Son died for your sins is no salvation at all if you will not show some *faith* by stepping into the light, by standing still in it and seeing yourself as God sees you. The crisis Jesus evokes here is God's gracious invitation to new life. It is love at ground zero. It is the only way God can save us in any realistic, living way. It is entry into the kingdom of God, nothing less than new birth.

So Jesus proclaims a here-and-now, do-it-yourself judgment day. The light has come into the world; people either flee from it or come to it. We make our own choices, our own judgments. We cannot blame God as some patriarchal ogre we cannot face. It is *ourselves* in the truth of God's light that we dread to face. The light is the warmth of God's love, but we cannot know it as love until we step into it and learn how to stay there, in Christ. It is a mortifying experience to stand still and see ourselves clearly. But it is also a new birth. The self that freely remains in the light is a fundamentally new self. It is the start of a new life in Christ.

The Son of Man comes to judge all humanity, including those who lived before Christ, and those who never heard the gospel, or heard and did not believe. John 3:16 seems to make salvation dependent upon believing in some doctrinal way in Jesus. Yet Christ the light of the world abides in every person (John 1:9). The gospel of Jesus Christ *lifts him up* (like the bronze serpent in verses 14–15) for all to see and believe. Yet the good news of the gospel is not *our* good news until we turn to the light and come into its truth. The light is the presence of Christ, named or unnamed. Faithful living in the truth of the light is more basic to salvation than believing this or that proposition about Christ. And yet, hearing the gospel and truly believing in Jesus *brings* us to the light, *induces* the crisis of decision and rebirth. So in John's gospel, salvation is paradoxical. It is predicated upon both the particular, historical person of Jesus Christ *and* a universal light, present to all people in every time and place. To choose between the exclusive claim of Jesus Christ or the universal truth of his light in all people is to slight the full truth as it is witnessed in the Fourth Gospel.

By the time this conversation ends, it has "led up" to that *anagogical, apocalyptic* (see these words defined in the Introduction) vista, where a conversation based in (literal or literary) *history* becomes our own conversation with Christ, grounded in *mystery*. Nicodemus is left with his challenge/invitation, and we have received our own. If we look down on Nicodemus as a flightless bird well below our level, we have missed the point. The Pharisee's problem is the same as the Christian's. Indeed, it is a *universal* human dilemma, but paradoxically most acute for *religious* persons, those of us *trying* to live in relationship to God.

Reflections from the Quaker Tradition

George Fox was the central figure in the beginnings of the Quaker movement. He had been like many of the Seekers Sarah Blackborow addressed in the passage quoted in Conversation 1. Fox went into deep crisis and depression at age nineteen. He went from one teacher, book and group to the next, looking for answers to his misery. Finally, in 1647, after four years of wandering,

> As I had forsaken all the priests, so I left the separate preachers also, and those called the most experienced people; for I saw there was none among them all that could speak to my condition. And when all my hopes in them and in all men were gone, so that I had nothing outwardly to help me, nor could tell what to do, then, Oh then, I heard a voice which said, "There is one, even Christ Jesus, that can speak to thy condition," and when I heard it my heart did leap for joy. . . . My desires after the Lord grew stronger, and zeal in the pure knowledge of God and of Christ alone, without the help of any man, book, or writing . . . and then the Lord did gently lead me along, and did let me see his love,

which was endless and eternal, and surpasseth the knowledge that men have in the natural state, or can get by history or books; and that love did let me see myself as I was without him. . . . I could see nothing but corruptions, and the life lay under the burden of corruptions. And when I was in the deep, under all shut up, I could not believe that I should ever overcome; my troubles, my sorrows, and my temptations were so great, that I thought many times I should have despaired, I was so tempted.

But when Christ opened to me how he was tempted by the same Devil, and had overcome him and bruised his head, and that through him and his power, light, and grace and spirit, I should overcome also, I had confidence in him. . . . Christ it was who had enlightened me, that gave me his light to believe in, and gave me hope, which is himself, revealed himself in me, and gave me his spirit and gave me his grace, which I found sufficient in the deeps and in weakness [Fox, 1952, pp. 11–12].

Fox finally was able to center his consciousness and his life in the presence of Christ, the light within him. The light let him see himself in his alienation from God. It let him see his own sin and corruption. But he recognized in this light of pure judgment the endless love of God. This parallels Jesus describing to Nicodemus God's love and God's judgment almost in the same breath. Fox's teaching in coming years centered on the presence of Christ as a guiding light and teacher. But note that the example of the historic Jesus is also crucial here. It guided him through the moment of impasse, where he could see only corruption and temptation to despair. Fox drew hope from the story of Christ's experience of temptation. In Christ he too could overcome. So Fox's experience of the light within was profoundly identified with the person of Jesus Christ and the witness of Scripture.

Fox's *Journal* goes on to narrate the light's profound transformation of his life over succeeding months. That experience shaped his spiritual counsel to Seekers still suffering bewilderment and despair. The Quaker movement gathered people who were transformed by the power of Christ's light in their consciences. Some of Fox's early epistles capture his style of personal counsel. Epistle #17 (1652) makes particular use of the imagery of Jesus' words to Nicodemus:

Dear Friends,—Prize your time, and the love of the Lord to your souls above all things; and mind that light in you, that shows you sin and evil.

Which checks you, when you speak an evil word, and tells you, that ye should not be proud, nor wanton, nor fashion yourselves like unto the world; for the fashion of this world passeth away. And if ye hearken to that, it will keep you in humbleness of mind, and lowliness of heart, and turn your minds within, to wait upon the Lord, to be guided by it; and bring you to lay aside all sin and evil, and keep you faithful to the Lord; and bring you to wait upon him for teaching, till an entrance thereof be made to your souls, and refreshment come to them from the presence of the Lord. There is your teacher, the light, obeying it; there is your condemnation, disobeying it. . . . Dear hearts, hearken to it, to be guided by it. For if ye love the light, ye love Christ; if ye hate that, ye hate Christ [Fox, 1831, 7:25].

The challenge is to stand still in the light, to let it show you the truth about yourself (perhaps more than you wish to see), and not to flee. Through steadfastness in that place of insight, the way forward is revealed, refreshment experienced, and power felt to live up to the Lord. In Epistle #10 (1652), Fox counsels,

Friends,—Whatever ye are addicted to, the tempter will come in that thing; and when he can trouble you, then he gets advantage over you, and then ye are gone. Stand still in that which is pure, after ye see yourselves; and then mercy comes in. After thou seest thy thoughts, and the temptations, do not think, but submit; and then power comes. Stand still in that which shows and discovers; and there doth strength immediately come. And stand still in the light, and submit to it, and the other will be hushed and gone; and then content[ment] comes. And when temptations and troubles appear, sink down in that which is pure and all will be hushed, and fly away. Your strength is to stand still, after ye see yourselves; whatsoever ye see yourselves addicted to, temptations, corruption, uncleanness, etc. then ye think ye shall never overcome. And earthly reason will tell you, what ye shall lose; hearken not to that, but stand still in the light that shows them to you, and then strength comes from the Lord, and help contrary to your expectation. Then ye grow up in peace, and no trouble shall move you. . . . [C]ome to stay your minds upon that spirit which was before the letter; here ye learn to read the scriptures aright. If ye do any thing in your own wills, then ye tempt God; but stand still in that power which brings peace [Fox, 1831, 7:20–21].

Fox's description of addiction may speak more compellingly to many today than the language of sin and corruption. Fox's counsel to remain still with an unpleasant insight, to linger in the negative moment, is counter-intuitive to most of us. We want to flee. Yet, Fox advises that this is precisely where we receive mercy, contentment, strength and peace. The meditation that closes this chapter is an opportunity to test that counsel.

Guided Conversation

The following is an exercise in remaining still in the light, in seeing more clearly the truth about yourself, and beginning again. Here, clarity comes not through heady problem-solving but through a felt, bodily sense. Christ dwells with us at a level below the mind and heart. Christ can redirect both mind and heart in powerful ways, but accomplishes it from below. Christ comes in the humble form of a servant.

As with all the meditations in this book, it is important to take time to be quiet. Find a quiet place to sit for twenty to thirty minutes or more. Sit in a comfortable but upright position. Still your body for a few moments. Feel yourself breathing; perhaps notice the pulse somewhere in your body. As you come to a place of quiet, calm awareness say, "Here I am."

Now, take time to survey what's happening in your life. What problems or unresolved questions are you facing? Consider a few briefly, calmly. Choose one you can feel somewhere in your body. Stay there with it. Don't get tangled up in it with thoughts and emotions. Just consider it, and observe your bodily response to it.

What word or phrase fits what you are feeling? Take some time with that. Wait until you find something that names the feeling and helps you stay in touch with it. Don't intensify the sense, just stay with it. Let the word and the sense resonate for a little while. (If you find yourself struggling with intense feelings or difficult thoughts, you may choose to stand up and walk away from the meditation. You may wish to return to it at another time.)

Now, ask why it feels this way. What is it about this situation in your life that gives you this feeling? Don't strive for an explanation so much as a few words that resonate with the sense in your body. Let your body tell you the truth of the matter. Be patient with yourself. The sense will fade at times, but your chosen word or phrase may help you return to it.

As you find the sense of the matter, you are coming into the light and learning to "stand," to remain still there. Ask Christ to teach you and lead you into the truth of this situation of life. Stay in the stillness as long as you can. Something helpful may come there. Or it may come only later, indirectly.

When the felt sense has passed, or you have run out of time to spend there, close with prayer. You might thank God for helping you see yourself and your situation more clearly. You may wish to ask God to continue teaching and leading you in this matter, and reaffirm your intention to return to this teachable place often.

CONVERSATION 3
A Woman of Samaria
John 4:1–26

The conversation with Nicodemus ends with no indication that Jesus has reached him. His reappearance at Jesus' burial (see John 19:39) indicates at least that he continued to be a sympathizer. Perhaps his expertise in religious matters is more impediment than aid to insight and rebirth. Perhaps the man-to-man dynamics of a conversation within a patriarchal religious context frustrate the conversation. In any case, this next conversation with a Samaritan woman goes much further.

4:1–15: Now when Jesus learned that the Pharisees had heard, "Jesus is making and baptizing more disciples than John"—although it was not Jesus himself but his disciples who baptized—he left Judea and started back to Galilee. But he had to go through Samaria. So he came to a Samaritan city called Sychar, near the plot of ground that Jacob had given to his son Joseph. Jacob's well was there, and Jesus, tired out by his journey was sitting by the well. It was about noon.

A Samaritan woman came to draw water, and Jesus said to her, "Give me a drink." (His disciples had gone to the city to buy food.) The Samaritan woman said to him, "How is it that you, a Jew, ask a drink of me, a woman of Samaria?" (Jews do not share things in common with Samaritans.) Jesus answered her, "If you knew the gift of God, and who it is that is saying to you, 'Give me drink,' you would have asked him, and he would have given you living water." The woman said to him, "Sir, you have no bucket, and the well is deep. Where do you get that living water? Are you greater than our ancestor Jacob, who gave us the well, and with his sons and his flocks drank from it?" Jesus said to her," Everyone who drinks of this water will be thirsty again, but those who drink of the water that I will give them will never be thirsty. The water that I will give will become in them a spring of water gushing up to eternal life." The woman said to him, "Sir, give me this water, so that I may never be thirsty or have to keep coming here to draw water."

The fame of Jesus is spreading. Word has it that he attracts and baptizes more disciples than does the Baptist. John pointedly clarifies that, although his disciples baptized, Jesus himself did not. Nevertheless, this mention implies a growing sense of sectarian competition, centering on the rite of baptism. (It is worth noting that in 1 Corinthians 1, Paul describes a similar competitive atmosphere at Corinth, making him glad he has baptized no one). Jesus opts to break the atmosphere of competition by leaving Judea for Galilee. Perhaps the move also weans his disciples from the rite of baptism, a subject that will not arise again in John's gospel.

On their way north through Samaria, Jesus and the disciples stop at Sychar (probably the site of the ancient Israelite city of Shechem). Jesus is left alone at a place called Jacob's well, as his disciples go to procure lunch. It is the noon hour—a time of full illumination—contrasting sharply with the nighttime encounter with Nicodemus. A local woman arrives to draw water and Jesus strikes up a conversation. When read in the light of the Old Testament, the scene has matrimonial overtones. Abraham's servant met Rebekah at a well at Aram-naharaim and arranged for the marriage of Abraham's son, Isaac (Gen. 24). Jacob met Rachel at a well at Haran (Gen. 29). Moses met Zipporah at a well in Midian (Exod. 2). Moreover, at the end of the preceding chapter (3:29), the Baptist refers to Jesus as the bridegroom. So literary motifs of betrothal and marriage accompany this conversation.

Thirsty from his journey, Jesus asks bluntly: "Give me a drink." The Samaritan woman snaps back, who does Jesus think he is, asking her for a drink? Indeed, with one terse request, Jesus has breached three boundaries. First, Jews and Samaritans have had a long history of ethnic hostility. More than five centuries earlier, Samaritans harassed the Jewish community returning from Babylon. The two groups had chafed at each other ever since. Second, for a Jewish man to speak to a Samaritan woman compounded the ethnic hostility with gender tension. Finally, although Samaritans shared the five books of Moses with Jews as Scripture, Jews considered them religiously corrupt and ritually unclean. So a Jew would not normally use a Samaritan's drinking vessel. Therefore, she responds to Jesus with incredulous contempt.

A kind of *frisson* is developing here, as in the early scenes of a Hollywood romantic comedy. The protagonists initially bristle at each other. Jesus responds with apparent masculine bravado: If you knew who you were talking to, you would ask me for a drink. I would give you living water. "Living" water in Greek usage would suggest flowing water, more refreshing than stagnant water from a well or cistern. But Jesus is already moving to another level, as he immediately did with Nicodemus. He has begun speaking of the Spirit. Like Nicodemus, she is still at the literal level when she reminds Jesus that he has no bucket. Does he think he is greater than "our ancestor Jacob, who gave us this well...?" "Our ancestor Jacob" may mean to acknowledge the common ancestry of Jews and Samaritans. She may be allowing for some common ground between herself and Jesus. But "gave us this well" no doubt refers to Samaritans only, for this is their territory. She doesn't yet understand Jesus' true intentions, but she meets and matches him point for point.

Jesus presses further: Drinking from this well soon leaves people thirsty again. But the water I give will never leave people thirsty again. It becomes within them a spring welling up to eternal life. She responds eagerly (or sarcastically?): Give me some of that! Very quickly we have moved from Jesus asking her for a drink, to Jesus offering to *give her* living water—water that actually wells up *within herself*. A number of boundaries—Jew versus Samaritan, man versus woman, outward/ physical versus inward/spiritual—have now been crossed or thrown into question.

> **4:16–26:** Jesus said to her, "Go call your husband, and come back." The woman answered him, "I have no husband." Jesus said to her, "You are right in saying, 'I have no husband', for you have had five husbands, and the one you have now is not your husband. What you have said is true!" The woman said to him, "Sir, I see that you are a prophet. Our ancestors worshiped on this mountain, but you say that the place where people must worship is in Jerusalem." Jesus said to her, "Woman, believe me, the hour is coming when you will worship the Father neither on this mountain nor in Jerusalem. You worship what you do not know; we worship what we know, for salvation is from the Jews. But the hour is coming, and is now here when the true worshipers will worship the Father in spirit and truth, for the Father seeks such as these to worship him. God is spirit, and those who worship him must worship in spirit and truth." The woman said to him, "I know that Messiah is coming"

(who is the Christ). "When he comes, he will proclaim all things to us." Jesus said to her, "I am he, the one who is speaking to you."

Suddenly, Jesus changes the subject. He asks her to go find her husband and bring him. She responds that she is unattached. Jesus commends her honesty, adding that she has had five husbands and is currently living with a man. Either she has led a colorful life, or Jesus speaks symbolically. There are various possible symbolisms involved here. Perhaps Jesus alludes to the Assyrian conquest of Samaria in 722 BCE. In 2 Kings 17:24 we are told that the Assyrians took many Israelites/Samaritans away into slavery. They replaced them with foreign colonists from five cities in the empire, who of course brought their pagan gods with them. If that is the implication here, then an earthly matter has again been transmuted into a spiritual one.

Jesus may simply be adapting here a popular Jewish gibe against Samaritans as a mixed group. (In Mark 7:27, when Jesus is approached by a Syrophoenician woman, he initially rebuffs her with a remark comparing Gentiles to mongrels.) But this Samaritan is undaunted. Whether Jesus is speaking of husbands, religions, or ethnicity, she perceives that he is a prophet, a man who sees through appearances. So she challenges Jesus to see past the old grudges between Jews and Samaritans. She leadingly notes that Samaritans have worshiped God for generations "on this mountain" (Mount Gerazim, within sight of the well), while Jews insist that people must worship in Jerusalem. In doing so, she has pointed out "the elephant in the living room," the central issue of conflict between Jews and Samaritans. But she has posed the matter in neutral terms.

Jesus responds to her good faith: "Woman, believe me, the hour is coming when you will worship the Father neither on this mountain nor in Jerusalem. You worship what you do not know; we worship what we know, for salvation is from the Jews. But the hour is coming, and is now here, when the true worshipers will worship the Father in spirit and truth, for the Father seeks such as these to worship him. God is spirit, and those who worship him must worship in spirit and truth." She has posed an *either/or* dilemma. He offers a *neither/nor* response. They must meet at this next level, neither his place nor hers but in spirit and truth. Indeed, the meeting has *already begun* ("is now here") with this conversation.

Through this exchange, John portrays in miniature the larger breakthrough of the Christian movement. The Acts of the Apostles describes the Gentile mission beginning with Jewish Christian outreach to Samaritans. That could not take place in earnest until after the death of Jesus, after the completion of his ministry to his own people. But this scene from the Gospel of John (together with the healing of the Syrophoenician woman's daughter in the Synoptic gospels) suggests that Jesus reached occasionally beyond even the margins of his own society. And in these few significant encounters, Gentiles demonstrated faith that apparently surprised Jesus. Think of the Roman centurion whose faith "amazed" him (Luke 7:9).

Women evidently acted as bridge-builders, significant co-initiators of that breakthrough. Their role at that pivotal moment in human history cannot be overestimated. Perhaps they were in a better position to see past the temple rituals at Jerusalem and the sacrifices on Mount Gerazim. As women they had *no role* and *less stake* in religious establishments. This Samaritan woman could grasp (more readily than his own disciples) what Jesus meant by a worship liberated from the ethnic and cultic loyalties of Jews and Samaritans. So, through conversations like this one, the gospel of Jesus Christ became an international, universalist network of conversations. Beginning in Samaria, in the first decades after Jesus' death, it quickly spread through the Greco-Roman world. Within the literary economy of his gospel, John sketches that larger, historic transformation: he moves quickly from Jesus calling his disciples, to the impasse with Nicodemus, to a breakthrough encounter with a Samaritan woman.

Still, *this* interfaith dialogue is not a mere exercise in multicultural good manners. Jesus states bluntly, "You worship what you do not know; we worship what we know, for salvation is from the Jews." His remark on Gentile *unknowing* at first sounds dismissive. But the conversation with Nicodemus has demonstrated acutely the problem of *knowing*! Jesus challenges Nicodemus to move beyond his inferential, intellectual knowledge, based upon expertise in the Scriptures. Still, Jesus by no means devalues the historic revelation to his own people, recorded in their Scriptures. He affirms that "salvation is from the Jews." But that salvation does not come by means that can be *grasped*. So, when it comes to worship in spirit and truth, something may be said for *not knowing*.

In these two conversations, Jesus has spoken of seeing and entering the kingdom of God, of coming to the light of judgment, and of living water welling up within a person. Now he prophesies a future worship in spirit and truth already beginning to take place. Such pronouncements have taken both Nicodemus and the Samaritan woman beyond the bounds of their knowledge. Worship in spirit and truth always stretches and ruptures our categories, expectations, hopes, and fears. When Jesus testifies that "God is spirit," he is not making a metaphysical statement. Likewise, when John the apostle testifies that "God is love" (1 John 4:16), he is not defining God. Both statements are about *the way* we know, worship, obey, and testify to God. That is, through love, through spirit and truth. Nicodemus can bring his biblical expertise to the realm of spirit and truth. But he must *yield* it, not wield it, there. The Samaritan woman may be able to enter that realm more easily than Nicodemus. But she must not be satisfied to remain in vague unknowing. There are specific truths to learn and explicit leadings to follow.

That unfolds next. The Samaritan again rises to the occasion. She answers, "I know that Messiah is coming. . . . When he comes, he will proclaim all things to us." With only the five books of Moses as their Scriptures, Samaritans did not adhere to the messianic promises of the Jewish prophetic tradition. But they would have known of Jewish messianic beliefs and expectations. So, because Jesus asserts that "salvation is from the Jews," she gropes for that term, intuiting that it pertains to the things Jesus prophesies. She combines it, however, with an end-time expectation that Samaritans shared with Jews. Based upon the prophecy of Moses in Deuteronomy 18:18, both groups expected a future prophet who would "proclaim all things" from God. Jesus responds with the crowning revelation of the conversation: "I am he, the one who is speaking to you." This emphatic "I am" will occur significantly several times in John's gospel. Evoking the divine name ("I am who I am," spoken to Moses from the burning bush in Exodus 3:14), Jesus asserts his identity with God.

Showing good faith at every turn, this unnamed woman has received a "mountain-top" revelation. She receives it *close* to "her" mountain, but in truth *far past* it. However, like so many such experiences, it quickly evaporates. "Just then his disciples came." Here-and-now lunch-time arrangements suddenly reassert mundane reality. She quickly realizes that her conversation with Jesus is over. But rather than glower at these Jewish men, she runs to tell her Samaritan neighbors. Soon she brings a whole crowd of people to meet Jesus. Like the disciples, she is an instant evangelist, witnessing at the edge of her own discovery. In this remarkable conversation between Jesus and an insightful Samaritan woman, a profound connection has been made. A kind of betrothal has indeed taken place, for an impending covenant bond between two estranged peoples in Christ.

Reflections from the Quaker Tradition

George Fox fluidly used language and imageries from the Gospel of John and many other books of Hebrew and Christian Scripture. For example, in a 1679 epistle to Friends, he used imagery from the conversation at Jacob's well to describe the experience of Christ:

> So believers do feel a living spring springing up in them to eternal life, from the fountain from whence it cometh. And . . . such may drink freely and eat freely of the bread and water of life, and do hunger and thirst no more, but eat and drink that which is eternal, which nourish them up to eternal life, and so bear heavenly fruits, to the praise of the eternal God [Fox, 1831, 8:167].

Like the Samaritan woman who engaged Jesus so vigorously, several outstanding women prophets and organizers helped advance the Quaker movement. And just as the Samaritan woman prefigures the opening of Samaria to the gospel after Jesus' death, Quaker women prophets, traveling in pairs, were often the first to open up new territory for their movement. Women first preached the Quaker gospel in tough Puritan strongholds such as Oxford. They were first to confront the Puritan establishment in Massachusetts. Mary Fisher, a domestic servant from Yorkshire, even traveled to Adrianople to preach to the Great Sultan of the Turkish Empire. She was generously received. But in the Christian world, early Quaker women were more often imprisoned or savagely whipped for their witness.

Margaret Fell, a member of the gentry in Lancashire, opened her home to George Fox and other Quaker preachers in 1652. She soon became coordinator for the early movement, making her home a base of operations. Like other early Friends, she believed that simple Quaker worship in silence was the worship in Spirit and Truth that Jesus had prophesied to the Samaritan woman. The Protestant Reformation had generated many liturgical forms, many competing practices of sacramental observance. George Fox complained that the Reformation and Counterreformation had reduced Christianity to "heaps and confusion." Each church and sect sat atop its own accumulation of doctrines and liturgies, its own Jerusalem or Gerazim. Many earnest Seekers of the day could no longer believe in of any of them.

Margaret Fell suffered four years of harsh imprisonment at Lancaster Castle for holding Quaker meetings for worship in her home at Swarthmoor Hall. During that imprisonment, in 1664, she published a tract titled, *A Call to the Universal Seed of God*. In it, she reflected on the conversation between Jesus and the Samaritan woman and proclaimed,

> God, being an invisible Spirit, hath placed his worship in the Spirit, and is removed from all visible things and all visible worships and offerings, and sacraments and temples, though God commanded them for a time, Christ Jesus hath fulfilled all, and removed them all, and hath proclaimed and given freely an everlasting Covenant of Light [p. 5].
>
> And so Men and People upon the face of the Earth ought to know the true and living God who is a spirit, and whose worship and fear is in the Spirit and in the truth in the inward parts [Jer. 31:33] by which eternal Spirit they come to be the temples of the living God [1 Cor. 3:16] [p. 10].
>
> Therefore hold fast your integrity, and stand fast in that liberty wherewith Christ hath made you free [Gal. 5:1], and be not entangled again with the beggarly Rudiments and carnal Ordinances which die of themselves . . . see that ye refuse not him that speaketh from heaven [Heb. 12:25] in your hearts [p. 16].

One enters into the covenant as one stands still in the light (see Fox's counsel in Conversation 2). In stillness, gathered worshippers become the temple of the living God, as each heart finds its center in Spirit and Truth.

In London, Mary Penington suffered many years of religious doubt. Her seeking brought her no peace or assurance of God's acceptance. She and her husband, Isaac, spent two years in conversation with Quakers before they began finding the peace they so desperately sought. Both were sophisticated urban intellectuals who had trouble accepting the simple truth as it was spoken by these rustics from the North. But as they worshipped with Friends, their hearts opened to that simplicity. By 1658, they began to adopt the plain speech, dress, and lifestyle of Friends, which was even more challenging for upperclass Londoners than it was for the rural Yorkshireman Luke Cock (see Conversation 1). Their friends and especially their families were deeply offended by their new, outlandish manners. Nevertheless, she writes,

> by taking up the cross, I received strength against many things which I had thought impossible to deny; but many tears did I shed and bitterness of soul did I experience, before I came thither [i.e., to the cross].... But oh! the joy that filled my soul in the first meeting ever held in my house at Chalfont. To this day I have a fresh remembrance of it. It was then the Lord enabled me to worship Him in that which was undoubtedly his own, and give up my whole strength, yea, to swim in the life which overcame me that day. Oh! long had I desired to worship Him with acceptation, and lift up my hands without doubting, which I witnessed that day in that assembly. I acknowledged his great mercy and wonderful kindness; for I could say, "This is it which I have longed and waited for, and feared I never should have experienced" [M. Penington, 1992, p. 45].

In Quaker silent worship, Penington felt herself swimming in the water that springs forth from within (remember the "watered" meeting to which Luke Cock referred). Both Fell and Penington took deep satisfaction in making their homes places of hospitality to traveling Quaker ministers, and places for organizational meetings—but most of all houses of worship. So, while early Quaker women prophets could be as courageous and confrontational as the Quaker men (and suffer as drastically for it) they also found hosting worship in their homes to be a powerful integration of their domestic and prophetic personas.

Guided Conversation

The following is an opportunity to experience Christ present within you as a well of living water. It is also an opportunity to meet someone else at that well.

As with all the meditations in this book, it is important to take time to be quiet. Find a quiet place to sit for twenty to thirty minutes or more. Sit in a comfortable but upright position. Still your body for a few moments. Feel yourself breathing; perhaps notice the pulse somewhere in your body. As you come to a place of quiet, calm awareness say, "Here I am."

Now take a moment to consider a personal acquaintance. Someone who adheres to a faith other than yours. Or perhaps someone who is non-religious, but whose personal integrity is clear to you. You may know several people that fit that description. Single out one you know fairly well, perhaps someone you've conversed with on spiritual matters.

Imagine that person with you right now. Does that person elicit in you admiration? Misgivings? Curiosity? Competition? Love? Imagining her or him with you right now, what would you like to say? Take a few moments to identify that sense.

Now can you sense the well of living water in that person? Does she or he seem to have a source of life and love, spirit and truth, to draw upon? Consider your acquaintance with that person. How have you sensed that source in them? Now take a few moments to consider what you would say to that person about the spiritual source within him or her. Just a phrase or two.

Next, take this imaginary encounter as an opportunity to see yourself. How do you draw from your own well? How do you find the living water? What activities take you there? Feel yourself there now, drinking from that well, satisfying the deepest thirst of your soul. Spend as long there as you wish. It is your source.

Finally, you may wish to thank God for the gift of living water. Feel the depth of your gratitude. Gratitude is one of the surest paths to the fountain. You may also wish to confess your ungenerous thoughts, words, or actions toward those with convictions different from your own. But return to your sense of gratitude. You may wish to reaffirm your intention to draw from that well, both with your Christian sisters and brothers, and with the strangers you meet at the well. Some of the unlikeliest conversations and friendships begin there.

CONVERSATION 4

'The Jews'
John 5:31–47

The Gospel of John is relentlessly negative in its portrayal of "the Jews," at least in their response to Jesus. Over the centuries, John's portrayal has been used to justify and perpetuate virulent anti-Judaism and even anti-Semitism. But when one examines the seventy instances in John's gospel, it becomes clear that *the Jews* is not a general religious and ethnic category. It refers more specifically to the religious and political authorities (and sometimes those under their sway) particularly around Jerusalem. Of course, Jesus and nearly all the characters in John's gospel are ethnically and religiously Jewish. So *the Jews* in John has more specific connotations. A modern-day equivalent might be found in African-American references to dominant white authority as *the man*, when the speakers themselves are no less men or women.

The Jews amounts to a specific instance of the more general term *the world* (Greek *kosmos*) in John. Jesus also uses *the world* pejoratively. Even God's love for the world (John 3:16) is not on account of worldly virtue. Readers sometimes conclude that John holds a negative (perhaps Gnostic) view of the material universe generally and human physical existence in particular. Yet, John's Prologue witnesses to the material world as the Word's creation. The noun in that case is not *kosmos*, but simply *panta* (all things). A careful reading of John's references to *the world* (*kosmos*) shows that he uses the word mainly to denote the realm of human consciousness and activity in the physical universe. It is not the material world as such but our "take" on it, and taking of it. *The world* is more than personal, subjective reality; it is also the social construction of reality in which we all participate. But most importantly, it is our consciousness of reality in alienation from the source and destiny of all reality. The Prologue states it succinctly: "He was in the world, and the world came into being through him; but the world did not know him" (1:10).

The conversations in John's gospel dramatize this problem of worldly non-recognition of Jesus. Even the disciples and the Samaritan woman struggle for clarity. *The Jews*, the religious and political authorities in John's gospel, epitomize *the world* of his specific time and place. Thus, John's Prologue presses the point of the world's non-recognition of Christ with the specific case of Jewish non-recognition: "He came to what was his own, and his own people did not accept him" (1:11). The problem for *the Jews* is one specific instance of human alienation generally. Every religious tradition (including Christian), every culture, every ethnic group falls into the same difficulties.

Traditionally, scholarship has often viewed John as a gospel written by Gentiles, particularly owing to its strong polemic against *the Jews*. But more recent scholarship emphasizes the Jewishness of the Fourth Gospel. The intensity of its conflicts arises from the spiraling conflict about Jesus within the Jewish community, spanning several decades following his death. No doubt, the historical Jesus did spark controversies with scribes, Pharisees and priests of his own day. But John has overlaid those with many subsequent controversies. The bitterness of John's portrayal of *the Jews* arises from the experience of Jewish Christians who were anathematized or even expelled from synagogue congregations. Hence, early generations of Jewish Christians wrote their own experience into these conversations. Likewise, the Gospel of John invites readers to bring their own experience to these same conversations.

The conversation we now explore is much less satisfying than the one we just finished. It is filled with acrimony and conflict. William Countryman (1994:46) calls such conversations in John the "obnoxious discourses." Jesus seems bent on alienating the alienated, insulting and jarring those who are comfortable with anything less than a direct encounter with the truth. What follows is barely a conversation at all but a one-sided polemic. But if we listen carefully, we hear Jesus offer his fellow Jews (and by implication, Christians too) a way to know him despite (but also through) their religious beliefs.

The following passage is only part of a long monologue by Jesus. It includes none of the brief interaction with Jewish authorities that sparked it. The longer monologue contains several related themes. I have included here only the section that addresses questions about the validity of Jesus' ministry. It is a highly condensed, almost systematic defense of Jesus' words and actions. It appears to be John's literary creation, reflecting decades of synagogue debate about Jesus. At the same time, however, some of these arguments might easily have been heard between Jesus and Jewish leaders of his day.

The present controversy arises from a miracle performed on the Sabbath. Jesus has healed a man long disabled by paralysis. The man then witnesses to (or informs against?) Jesus before the authorities. When *the Jews* confront Jesus about his Sabbath-breaking act, Jesus simply replies, "My Father is still working, and I also am working." Here Jesus draws upon the Jewish teaching that God works on the Sabbath, in order to sustain the creation. But claiming such intimacy, equality, and freedom with God scandalizes his hearers. Jesus adds that, as the Son, he does nothing on his own. He does only what he sees the Father doing. This an image of apprenticeship, a relationship Jesus perhaps knew for a time with his earthly father in Nazareth. "The Father loves the Son and shows him all that he himself is doing."

To these jaw-dropping statements he adds, "Very truly, I tell you, anyone who hears my word and believes him who sent me has eternal life, and does not come under judgment, but has passed from death to life" (5:24). Jesus induces a crisis. He takes a serious question of Sabbath-infraction and rapidly escalates matters with the highest theological claims. He has their undivided attention.

5:31–47: "If I testify about myself, my testimony is not true. There is another who testifies on my behalf, and I know that his testimony to me is true. You sent messengers to John, and he testified to the truth. Not that I accept such human testimony, but I say these things so that you may be saved. He was a burning and shining lamp, and you were willing to rejoice for a while in his light. But I have a testimony greater than John's. The works that the Father has given me to complete, the very works that I am doing, testify on my behalf that the Father has sent me. And the Father who sent me has himself testified on my behalf. You have never heard his voice or seen his form, and you do not have his word abiding in you, because you do not believe him whom he has sent.

"You search the scriptures because you think that in them you have eternal life; and it is they that testify on my behalf. Yet you refuse to come to me to have life. I do not accept glory from human beings. But I know that you do not have the love of God in you. I have come in my

Father's name, and you do not accept me; if another comes in his own name, you will accept him. How can you believe when you accept glory from one another and do not seek the glory that comes from the one who alone is God? Do not think that I will accuse you before the Father; your accuser is Moses, on whom you have set your hope. If you believed Moses, you would believe me, for he wrote about me. But if you do not believe what he wrote, how will you believe what I say?"

Jesus addresses the crucial question of *verifiability*: how can he establish these outrageous assertions as truth? He readily admits that, taken alone, his statements about himself have no validity. But he claims to have confirming witnesses, a method of verification established in the laws of Moses. Two or three confirming witnesses are required to establish an accusation, according to Numbers 35:30 and Deuteronomy 17:6 (also see John 8:17). He simply asserts, "There is another who testifies on my behalf, and I know that his testimony is true." This "another" turns out to be four different witnesses, perhaps all understood as confirmations provided by the Father. It is important to look at each one.

First, Jesus cites the testimony of John the Baptist. We have already noted his witness to Jesus as the Lamb of God. Jesus himself does not accept human testimony, but he raises it for the sake of his hearers, "that you may be saved." After all, for a while they had rejoiced at the Baptist's preaching. The Baptist represents the testimony of the prophets, those who receive and communicate God's Word to the community of faith.

But Jesus quickly moves on, for "I have a testimony greater than John's." The works the Father has given Jesus to perform are the *second* confirming witness. These include the healing he has just performed. Such acts are signs intended to draw men and women to Jesus and confirm his teaching.

Third, the Father himself testifies on Jesus' behalf, by the Word abiding within men and women. John's Prologue has already testified that this Word is the light and life that enlightens every one. But here Jesus denies that his hearers have the Father's Word abiding in them, because they do not believe the one whom the Father has sent. In short, the testimony of Jesus is intended to awaken men and women to the Word, the witness of God in themselves, while the Word also confirms the witness and works of Jesus. But where the Word is ignored or repressed, it is effectively absent.

Fourth, the Scriptures testify to Jesus. Here lies the greatest irony: these religious leaders believe that they are saved by their study of Scripture. Yet they fail to recognize the one to whom the Scriptures point. Therefore, their assurance of life is hollow, false. They believe they can wield Scriptural authority by citing the opinions of learned scribes and other leaders like themselves on a given question (as scholars still do today). They receive authority, that is, "glory," from one another, trading it around in a self-serving manner. By contrast, Jesus accepts no glory from human authorities. He speaks only in the name of the Father, upon divine authority. He thus breaks with the "cosa nostra" of religious authority, deeply offending his hearers.

Now Jesus turns the tables of judgment against his accusers: "Do not think that I will accuse you before the Father; your accuser is Moses, on whom you have set your hope. If you believed Moses, you would believe me, for he wrote about me." Once again, Jesus claims to be the latter-day figure prophesied by Moses in Deuteronomy 18:18. "But if you do not believe what he wrote, how will be you believe what I say?" With an astonishing twist, Jesus suggests that his hearers are alienated even from the Scriptural authority they hold so dear.

As in his conversations with Nicodemus and the Samaritan woman, the point of departure here is a mundane perception of matters. In this case, the authorities have laid hold of a healing act as a breach of Sabbath regulations. They are applying the law topically, circumstantially. Jesus immediately moves the conversation to another level. In rapid succession, he has called his witnesses. He has cited the most recognized prophetic figure of the day, John the Baptist; he has described his miracles and healings as prophetic signs intended to provoke faith; he has invoked the self-authenticating witness of God's Word within the individual; and finally, he has called upon Moses, the prophets, and all the Scriptures, claiming that they foretold his coming.

This confrontation with the authorities is nearly a monologue. However, the witnesses Jesus invokes *themselves* constitute an interaction, a *conversation* of testimonies that establishes the truth. As suggested earlier, this passage probably represents something of Jesus' own confrontation with the authorities of his day. But it also voices the arguments Jewish Christians made in synagogue debates after Jesus' death. Finally, it articulates the Christian community's internal conversation of faith.

The community's understanding of Christ continued to develop through the interaction of memories of Jesus, the remembered testimony of the Baptist, reflection upon Scripture, and the Word of God abiding in their hearts. All these were animated by the Spirit of Truth. In other words, Jesus presents here a *hermeneutic*, a framework for interpretation, for ongoing prophetic discernment and community conversation.

So we find that questions of faith and practice are discerned not upon the authority of a single source, but through the interaction of multiple sources, as communities struggle to know and do God's will together. That interactive framework makes the conversation of faith possible and fruitful in changing circumstances. Whether we are "the Jews," "the Christians," or whatever category of "the world," we struggle with problems of alienation. We fail to recognize the person of Christ within ourselves, in others, and even the historical Jesus. We attach ourselves to favorite Scriptures, beliefs and practices, thinking that truth and salvation abide there. But the conversation of faith, sometimes painfully jarring like the one we have just heard, keeps shaking us loose from idolatrous certainties.

Reflections from the Quaker Tradition

In the Introduction to this book, we heard George Fox observe that Christians of his day often viewed the rejection of Jesus as a specifically Jewish betrayal. They also assumed that Paul's critique of legalism applied only to the laws of Moses. But Fox suggested that such assumptions are symptomatic of the same human alienation that both Jesus and Paul exposed. When people "came to look into themselves, and with the light of Christ thoroughly to search themselves, they might see enough of this in themselves; and then the cry could not be, it is he, or they, as before, but I and we are found in these conditions."

It is important to see Fox's point in its historical context. The Quaker movement arose at the end of the Reformation, when competing claims to Christian orthodoxy had subverted the Protestant hope to regain "primitive Christianity revived." Doctrinal debate had eclipsed spiritual experience for many. The Quaker movement attempted to draw people back to a direct awareness of Christ's presence as a guiding, teaching, and redeeming light in the heart. But that aim necessitated a vigorous confrontation with the reigning orthodoxies of Puritanism. People needed to be shaken loose from doctrinaire religion, what early Friends called "profession without possession." Hence, early Friends engaged in many "obnoxious discourses" with their Puritan contemporaries. They routinely denounced the clergy during parish Church services. In streets and marketplaces, they decried the hypocrisy and superficial piety of many rank-and-file Church-goers.

The name "Quaker" was a derisive nickname, referring to the shaking that passed in waves through their meetings for worship. Names they preferred for themselves were "Children of the Light" and "Friends of the Truth." They befriended truth as they encountered the light within, God's living word abiding in the heart, the indwelling love of God. As the young Fox began to ground his awareness and his life in the light of Christ, it first showed him the darkness and alienation in his own heart. Then it revealed the varieties of alienation in people around him.

> And ... the Lord shewed me that the natures of those things which were hurtful without were within, in the hearts and minds of wicked men. The natures of dogs, swine, vipers, of Sodom and Egypt, Pharaoh, Cain, Ishmael, Esau, etc. The natures of these things I saw within, though people had been looking without. And I cried to the Lord, saying "Why should I be thus, seeing I was never addicted to commit those evils?" And the Lord answered that it was needful I should have a sense of all conditions, how else should I speak to all conditions; and in this I saw the infinite love of God. I saw also that there was an ocean of darkness and death, but an infinite ocean of light and love, which flowed over the ocean of darkness. And in that also I saw the infinite love of God; and I had great openings. And as I was walking by the steeplehouse side, in the town of Mansfield, the Lord said unto me, "That which people do trample upon must be thy food." And as the Lord spoke he opened it to me how that people and professors did trample upon the life, even the life of Christ was trampled upon; and they fed upon words and fed one another with words, but trampled upon the life, and trampled underfoot the blood of the Son of God, which blood was my life, and they lived in their airy notions, talking of him [Fox, 1952, p. 19].

So Fox viewed the different characters of the Bible as representations of different natures of alienation from God. It was overwhelming to feel intimately so many varieties of darkness. His vision of an ocean of darkness approximates John's use of the term, *the world*. But his vision of an ocean of light and love gave him courage to face the darkness. Fox's great gift became his ability to discern the spiritual conditions of various people and lead them to the hidden treasure within, the food "which people do trample upon." (Recall Sarah Blackborow's counsel in Conversation 1, to Seekers who had listened to so many teachers but not the teacher within.)

Many years later, after Fox's death, Margaret Fell recalled the first time she heard him preach, in the parish church at Ulverston. After the priest had finished, Fox was given permission to speak. Fell vividly remembered him saying,

> The Scriptures were the prophets' words and Christ's and the Apostles' words, and what, as they spoke, they enjoyed and possessed, and had it from the Lord: And said, Then what had any to do with the Scriptures, but as they came to the Spirit that gave them forth. You will say, Christ saith this, and the Apostles say this; but what canst thou say? Art thou a Child of the Light, and hast thou walked in the Light, and what thou speakest, is it inwardly from God? etc. This opened me so, that it cut me to the Heart; and then I saw clearly, we were all wrong. So I sat down in my Pew again, and cried bitterly: and I cried in my Spirit to the Lord, We are all Thieves, we are all Thieves; we have taken the Scriptures in Words and know nothing of them in our selves [Garman, et. al. 1996, p. 235].

Obnoxious confrontations like this one often led listeners to spontaneous acts of violence against young Fox. But these incidents also drew out tender souls like Fell, who knew they had been rightly discerned. That devastating insight led to weeks or months of deep struggle, as individuals saw themselves clearly for the first time and allowed the light to rebuild their lives. The letters of counsel quoted in Conversation 2 are examples of Fox's guidance, teaching earnest Seekers to stand still in the light and not flee its revelation. As one stands still and waits upon the Lord's teaching, the power is received to live a pure life.

But again following the conversation of Jesus with his critics, early Friends emphasized that their works, their actions, were their most eloquent witness. Fox exhorted Friends to "let your lives preach," to be the same in life as in words. Life lived in the light is a living testimony to the truth. Early Friends evolved a set of "testimonies," countercultural behaviors they believed communicated truth to the world around them. These included plain speaking, the refusal to use flattering titles, to engage in banal, unnecessary conversation or to barter. They adopted plainness of dress and simplicity of lifestyle. They refused to use violence or participate in military conflict. In Conversations 1 and 3, we heard of the struggles Luke Cock and Mary Penington endured in adopting these testimonies, which most contemporaries viewed as obnoxious, uncivil behavior.

In the twentieth century, Friends distilled these specific Quaker behavioral testimonies into general principles: *simplicity, peace, integrity, community, equality*. Modern Friends challenge themselves and one another to adapt these general principles of testimony to the specific circumstances of life. The contemporary British Quaker writer John Punshon observes,

> Inwardly, [the testimonies] are our guide to the nature of our Creator, the source of our inspiration, the medium of our understanding, the particular mystical path of Quakerism, our way to God. Externally, they are our guide to life, a sign of divine love for creation, the means of our prophetic witness. They therefore take their meaning from the highest reality we know [Punshon, 1990, p. 94].

Indeed, there is a sacramental quality to this attempt to find outward, ethical expressions of the inward mystery we have come to know and follow.

Guided Conversation

The following is an opportunity to reflect on a recent action. This meditation is more complex than the preceding ones, because it involves an interaction with Scripture, action, the figure of Jesus, and the witness of God within you.

> As with all the meditations in this book, it is important to take time to be quiet. Find a quiet place to sit for twenty to thirty minutes or more. Sit in a comfortable but upright position. Still your body for a few moments. Feel yourself breathing; perhaps notice the pulse somewhere in your body. As you come to a place of quiet, calm awareness say, "Here I am."
>
> Now consider a recent action you've taken, in responding to a problem or situation in your life. Has the action changed the situation in some way? If so, how? Has the action changed your perception of yourself

or others involved? If so, how? Has the action changed the way others respond to you? If so, how? Take a few moments to reflect upon what has changed because of (or simply along with) your action.

Now, take your perceptions and offer them up to the witness of God within. Do you feel any regrets? If so, where exactly did you "miss the mark"? You could ask for God's forgiveness. Do you feel you need to ask the forgiveness of others? If so, ask God to guide you in that. Or do you feel a sense of rightness in your action? If so, what about your action "hit the mark"? You could thank God for the strength and guidance to do a good thing. Are there others you would like to thank?

Now, consider what in Scripture might "speak" to that experience. It's difficult to predict where this question may lead. Just follow your heart. Does a certain verse echo inside you? Or does a certain image, character, or story resonate with your experience? More than one may come to mind. But settle on one that seems especially resonant. Sit with that resonance for a few moments. Let its truth arise in its own way. Let the Scripture witness to you its perspective on your experience. Is there a word or phrase that describes the connection? Listen quietly. Receive its truth without grasping at it.

Now, imagine the figure of Jesus sitting next to you. Look at the experience as you sit beside Jesus. What do you sense Jesus thinking or feeling about it? Is there a word of phrase that comes to you from Jesus about it? Linger a moment here.

Finally, consider: has this meditation revealed to you any new meaning in the Scripture that came to you? Has it shifted something in your relationship to God's witness in you? Has it renewed your sense of friendship with Jesus? Does it suggest a leading toward some further action? Take a few moments to savor the meditation. You may wish to give thanks for any new insights or encouragement received.

Recurring conversation between three or four persons constantly alters the dynamics between them, and they grow in a particular way through that conversation. Similarly, you will find that meditations like this one will alter and develop your partnership with the figure of Jesus, your reading of Scripture, your sensitivity to the witness of God in your heart, and the way you act in the world. The conversation continues, the give-and-take evolves.

A Hungry Crowd
John 6:25–40; 51–55

J esus keeps moving. New conversations advance his ministry. He is back again in Galilee, as the Feast of Passover approaches. His miraculous signs have attracted large crowds that follow him everywhere. They even follow him up a mountainside. Responding to their physical hunger, Jesus miraculously feeds five thousand seekers on five barley loaves and two fish. With the Passover near, the people are prone to find parallels between this miracle and the manna God provided the Israelites in the wilderness. So they exclaim that Jesus must be the prophet Moses said would come. Moreover, the Passover-Exodus story perennially rekindles hopes for political liberation. So when Jesus senses the crowd may forcibly make him their king, he withdraws further up the mountain by himself.

That evening, the disciples get into a boat and start back across the Sea of Galilee to Capernaum. But the sea is rough that night. As they struggle to get across, they see Jesus coming across on the water. He tells them not to fear. As they take him into the boat, they suddenly find themselves arriving on the other shore. Exodus overtones (the crossing of the Red Sea) accompany this story as well. Our passage takes up with the crowd seeking Jesus the next day in Capernaum.

> **6:25–34:** When they found him on the other side of the sea, they said to him, "Rabbi, when did you come here?" Jesus answered them, "Very truly, I tell you, you are looking for me, not because you saw signs, but because you ate your fill of the loaves. Do not work for the food that perishes, but for the food that endures for eternal life, which the Son of Man will give you. For it is on him that God the Father has set his seal." Then they said to him, "What must we do to perform the works of God?" Jesus answered them, "This is the work of God, that you believe in him whom he has sent." So they said to him, "What sign are you going to give us then, so that we may see it and believe you? What

work are you performing? Our ancestors ate the manna in the wilderness; as it is written, 'He gave them bread from heaven to eat.'" Then Jesus said to them, "Very truly, I tell you, it was not Moses who gave you the bread from heaven, but it is my Father who gives you the true bread from heaven. For the bread of God is that which comes down from heaven and gives life to the world." They said to him, "Sir, give us this bread always."

The people are puzzled: they had seen his disciples enter a boat without Jesus the evening before. So their first question is, how did he get here? Like the disciples' query in Conversation 1 ("Where are you staying?"), this question implies more than the crowd consciously intends. Jesus brushes aside their mundane concerns and draws them toward another level. He knows they didn't really see the sign he had performed in feeding them yesterday. Or more exactly, they didn't see *where the sign was pointing.* If it pointed anywhere for them, it was simply toward more bread today, and tomorrow. These are agrarian peasants, after all. Many of them live a hand-to-mouth existence. So Jesus remarks that they seek him again today not because they saw signs but because they ate their fill of loaves. Jesus *gave them bread*, but they *took it as loaves.* They grasped the *commodity*, the *form*, without perceiving the *substance.*

Jesus urges the crowd not to work for food that perishes but for food that endures to eternal life. Indeed, the Son of Man gives the latter (it cannot be earned). But the crowd focuses on working rather than receiving. They ask, what "works of God" must they do to obtain this imperishable food. Jesus ironically turns the phrase around, giving it an opposite meaning. The "work of God" is to believe in the Son. It is not work they must perform but a work that *God* accomplishes in them, the gift of faith. So the bread Jesus promises is neither the commodity of loaves, nor is it obtained through their commodified labor (such as gainful employment or observing the laws of Moses). Rather, the work of God *through* them produces the food that endures.

Apparently, the crowd at least understands that Jesus is the one sent by God, the one in whom they are to believe. So they ask, what work will he perform, that they should believe in him? They remind Jesus that Moses provided their ancestors manna in the wilderness. That was a daily event. So yesterday's miracle is only yesterday's miracle. What about today? Again, the crowd is mired in a worldly perspective of past and present, of daily installments of life. Jesus responds that it was not Moses who gave "bread from heaven." God *gives true bread from heaven*. Just as he tries to shift their focus from commodity to substance, Jesus also aims to shift their frame of reference from the past glories of the Exodus and from yesterday's miracle, to the eternally present work of God. He hopes to refocus their eyes into the eternal, heavenly dimension of their temporal, mundane present. But again they miss it. They simply ask Jesus to provide yesterday's bread every day. They request not the eternal, immeasurable gift but an indefinite repetition of goods.

> **6:35-40:** Jesus said to them, "I am the bread of life. Whoever comes to me will never be hungry, and whoever believes in me will never be thirsty. But I said to you that you have seen me and yet do not believe. Everything that the Father gives me will come to me, and anyone who comes to me I will never drive away; for I have come down from heaven, not to do my own will, but the will of him who sent me. And this is the will of him who sent me, that I should lose nothing of all that he has given me, but raise it up on the last day. This is indeed the will of my Father, that all who see the Son and believe in him may have eternal life; and I will raise them up on the last day."

Jesus now states the matter emphatically: "I am the bread of life. Whoever comes to me will never be hungry; and whoever believes in me will never be thirsty." This is another major "I am" statement. Each time Jesus enunciates it, he claims the eternal dimension of his identity, his equality with the Father. God had revealed *unpredicated* being to Moses on Mount Sinai through the divine name, "I am that I am." In saying "I am the bread of life," Jesus does not predicate his being as "bread." Rather, he suggests that eternal, spiritual nourishment is one way we can experience him.

In what follows, we shall see that Jesus Christ is the bread of life in two senses. First, Jesus speaks of bread as *divine revelation and guidance*. Later, he describes bread as the *sustenance of life*, or *life itself*. These are two aspects of one reality.

There is strong Old Testament precedent for describing God's guidance or teaching as bread. In Proverbs 9:5-6, the feminine figure of Wisdom invites all to "Come, eat of my bread and drink of the wine I have mixed; Lay aside immaturity and live, and walk in the way of insight." Similarly, Isaiah prophesies God's offer: "Why do you spend your money for that which is not bread, and your labor for that which does not satisfy? Listen carefully to me, and eat what is good, and delight yourselves in rich food. Incline your ear, and come to me; listen so that you may live" (55:2–3). In both cases, bread figures as revelation, the way of God's wisdom.

Jesus builds upon these wisdom and prophetic traditions, but goes still further. Verses 37–40 reframe the conversation, from Moses to Adam, from Exodus to creation and fall. The parallels and contrasts between Genesis 2–3 and John 6 are striking. In Genesis 2:17, God warns: "of the tree of the knowledge of good and evil you shall not eat, for in the day that you eat of it you shall die." In John 6:50, Jesus promises, "This is the bread that comes down from heaven, so that one may eat of it and not die." In Genesis 3:21 God decides that Adam must be driven out of the garden; otherwise, "He might reach out his hand and take also from the tree of life, and eat and live forever." In John 6:51 Jesus promises, "Whoever eats of this bread will live forever." In Genesis 3:24 God drives man and woman from the garden. In John 6:37 Jesus promises, "Anyone who comes to me I will never drive away."

These literary precedents and parallels are intended to lead us to an encounter with Christ. Jesus promises an insight that takes us beyond the ambivalent consciousness of good and evil that deadens human life. The serpent lured Eve and Adam into a fixation that stunts and kills. By tempting them to eat the one forbidden fruit, the serpent created the first "it," the first desirable commodity, the first occasion of envy and greed. Hence, the hungry crowd chases after Jesus for more loaves. But Jesus uses the occasion to offer a way past "it," a way to move beyond desire, envy, greed, and anxiety over obtaining the next "it." He offers a way back to the garden. Or rather, he offers himself as a way into the heavenly realm that is already present.

Like bread, knowledge is prone to objectification, to becoming "it." We saw in Conversation 4 authoritative knowledge of Scripture wielded by the Jewish authorities. They *grasped, comprehended* the particulars of the Torah. But that very knowledge prevented them from recognizing and believing in the one to whom the Scriptures point. By contrast, Jesus alludes to Jeremiah's prophecy that God's law shall be written upon human hearts, so that "They shall all be taught by God" (Jer. 31:34;

John 6:45). Again, this revelation of Christ, this shift in the order of knowledge, is no mere change of opinion. It is life itself.

Themes such as the Prophet-like-Moses, the prophecy of Jeremiah, and redemption from fallen existence are all *eschatological*: that is, focused on "last things," "the end." Eschatology is more overt in the first three gospels, where Jesus speaks more about the future (as in Mark 13, for example). In the Fourth Gospel, questions of "the end" are often refocused in terms of entering eternal life here and now. But even in John, Jesus does not ignore future hope entirely. While he offers eternal life as a present reality, he does not deny human mortality. So his offer of eternal life now is complemented by his promise of resurrection: "I will raise them up on the last day" (6:40, 44). But his emphasis remains upon the opportunity of the present. The hope of the resurrection is grounded in entering eternal life now.

Indeed, there is a mortal implication in Jesus' claim to be the Bread of Life. *Jesus becomes "It"* to those who still do not understand, who do not follow his signs into the truth. We saw a dark foreshadowing of this problem earlier. When the crowd acclaimed Jesus as the Prophet-like-Moses, they were ready to forcibly make him their king. Jesus saw that movement developing and withdrew. Later, he would escape an angry crowd ready to stone him (John 8:59). He evaded arrest "because his hour had not yet come" (John 7:39, 44). But his eventual arrest and death appear implicitly on the horizon with this conversation on the Bread of Life, making it the fulcrum in the Gospel of John.

> **6:51–55:** "I am the living bread that came down from heaven. Whoever eats of this bread will live forever; and the bread that I will give for the life of the world is my flesh." The Jews then disputed among themselves, saying, "How can this man give us his flesh to eat?" So Jesus said to them, "Very truly, I tell you, unless you eat the flesh of the Son of Man and drink his blood you have no life in you. Those who eat my flesh and drink my blood have eternal life, and I will raise them up on the last day; for my flesh is true food and my blood is true drink."

As the conversation continues, there is grumbling among "the Jews," religious leaders among the crowd. Literarily, it echoes the grumbling of the Israelites against Moses in the wilderness. But it also prefigures the lethal conflict ahead. First, they question his claims to come from heaven: "Is not this Jesus, the son of Joseph, whose father and mother we know?" (6:42). His earthly origins are well known here in Galilee, making his claims sound ludicrous. But again, his words are mistakenly heard in mundane terms.

Soon after, Jesus says, "and the bread that I will give for the life of the world is my flesh" (6:51). Here he alludes to his physical death. Again, the authorities are incredulous: "How can this man give us his flesh to eat?" (6:52). At this point, Jesus is pushing even his disciples past their limits. Many leave him that day (6:66). Jesus asks the twelve core disciples if they are leaving too. Even Simon Peter is barely holding on when he replies, "Lord, to whom can we go?" (6:68). These developments foreshadow not only the clash with religious authority that will send Jesus to Pilate for execution. They also hint at the scattering of disciples at the scene of Jesus' arrest. In the last verse of this scene (6:71), Judas Iscariot receives his first explicit mention.

By becoming "It"—especially near the Passover—Jesus focuses human desire and Jewish expectation upon himself. It overwhelms the fragile faith of even his closest friends. It also invites more hostile witnesses to indulge their worst fears about him as a blasphemer, a seducer of the people, a contagion of religious pollution and political upheaval. Jesus provokes upon himself the *scapegoat* impulse that permeates all communities. That is, he invites both power elites and restive mobs to focus their respective control anxieties and chronic dissatisfactions upon a controversial or vulnerable individual who can be blamed for their troubles. Through the social catharsis of sacrificing a victim, they may achieve new social solidarity and make peace among themselves (at least until the next crisis arises). In some cases, the victim is remembered with continuing hostility. In other cases, communities may elevate the victim to divine status. We know from experience that being "it" is dangerous. Being "it" may mean finding oneself the object of popular desire. Think, for example, of Princess Diana, literally hounded to death. Or being "it" may mean becoming the pariah, the "goat," shunned by all—until or unless one can "put the tag" on someone else. Either way, "it" is dangerous.

Jesus makes himself "It" fully understanding the price he will pay. He is willing to be "It," the ultimate sign, even at the cost of his life. He does so in order to invite all into communion with God, to abide in a life beyond all "its." Here we enter more fully into the second sense of Christ as bread: *life*. Verses 51–58 have strong overtones easily associated with the rite of communion, or Eucharist. Jesus invites his hearers to eat his flesh and drink his blood. Indeed, he stresses that one *must* do this in order to have life. The words stand out in John's gospel, particularly since his last supper with the disciples contains no mention of bread and wine, no "institution" of a Lord's Supper. Why does John allow the sacramental words of Jesus to remain ambiguous?

Possibly, John and the community that formed around him had already begun moving away from the Lord's Supper as a ritual enactment. We have already seen the ambiguity John creates regarding baptism: the disciples of Jesus baptized, but Jesus himself did not. It is not even clear in John that Jesus was baptized by John the Baptist. We have also seen that Jesus moves every conversation away from earthly matters, including elements such as water and bread, to more spiritual levels of meaning. Possibly, John lived long enough to witness the outward, ritual use of sacraments become a new "it" in Christian communities. That is, he saw bread and wine become *fetishized* as saving elements. Perhaps John did not want to reject the use of outward elements of water, bread, and wine; but he was concerned not to give them saving status either. Or perhaps he simply recalls how it was with Jesus.

This is a plausible surmise regarding the Eucharistic ambiguity in John. But I should admit to my viewpoint as a Quaker. Quakers (Friends) have traditionally renounced the use of outward elements in baptism and communion. Nevertheless, we affirm baptism and communion as necessary, life-giving spiritual realities. The early Quaker movement emerged as a final fruition of the Spiritualist stream of the Reformation, which consistently emphasized *inward experience* and *ethical expression* over outward ritual. That emphasis merits a place in any Christian conversation on sacraments. The genius of the Gospel of John lies in the space it allows for both spiritualist and ritualist interpretations.

To conclude, let us return to the point of departure for this entire conversation. The day before, Jesus had fed five thousand hungry Galileans. Given the mystical emphasis in John, it is easy to forget that the signs Jesus performs are *acts of loving concern*. Jesus had compassion upon a crowd of people that had pursued him into the wilderness.

He fed them physical bread. Of course, the act pointed to a greater, mystical reality, which is primary for us, since we were not there. But *it was a good thing in itself*. Jesus *gave thanks* (the Greek verb is *eucharistein*) and distributed the bread and fish. His *sacramental* act consisted in his *humanitarian* act. As with the healing of the paralytic noted in the preceding Conversation (and the healing of the blind man in the following Conversation), the miraculous aspect of these stories should not distract us. We may choose to insist that these stories are literally true, historical events. Or we may prefer a literary approach that opts for their symbolic meaning. But let us not miss their ethical-sacramental meaning.

Moreover, these stories of Jesus feeding and healing people are meant to inspire us to undertake similar actions. Our own humanitarian acts are sacramental signs of God's universal love. Moreover, they spark many of our most important conversations. Recall the Son of Man bridging heaven and earth (see Conversation 1). The angels descending to earth communicate not only the *words* of God's love but the *works* as well. Like Jesus, we may find the higher intention of our actions lost among various 'its' we supply. But just as Jesus broke and distributed the few loaves and fish available, we do what we can for others with what's available. We have no control over the results, or whether people understand our intention or not. In some cases, we may incur personal risk in being generous, as Jesus did in making himself "It." But "servants are not greater than their master" (John 13:16). When offered in love and with thanksgiving, every "it" is good in itself (note similarly 1 Tim. 4:4–5).

Reflections from the Quaker Tradition

In Conversation 4, we noted that competing orthodoxies finally defeated the Reformation project to renew primitive Christian faith and practice. Similarly, sacramental controversies sparked nagging debates and outright wars in that period. When I was in seminary in the early 1970s, one of my New Testament professors was Raymond Brown, a Catholic priest and renowned interpreter of the Gospel of John. (His massive commentary on John has been the primary resource for my research.) In a conversation with him, I mentioned that I was a Quaker.

He responded by reflecting on all the blood that was shed during the Protestant Reformation and Catholic Counter-Reformation over doctrines and sacraments. He said it wasn't surprising that, by the middle of the seventeenth century, at least one group took up a non-credal, non-sacramental, and pacifist position.

Of course, the Quaker position isn't actually non-sacramental but an inward, experiential understanding of baptism and communion. Friends do not criticize other groups for their ritual observance of the sacraments. But it carries the danger of substituting for the inward reality that it symbolizes. The outward symbol may stand in the way of the inward reality. Hence, George Fox challenged those who eat and drink in remembrance of Christ's death: "but will you come no nearer to Christ's death than to take bread and wine in remembrance of his death? For after you have eaten in remembrance of his death, then you must come into his death and die with him if you will live with him" [quoted in Gwyn (1986), p. 167].

Much early Quaker spiritual counsel was devoted to helping people "come into" Christ's death, in order to live more intimately with Christ. We saw in Conversation 2 Fox's advice to stand still in Christ's light, to let the light reveal one's darkness, alienation, and sin. Isaac Penington was another great spiritual guide among early Friends. Several of his tracts and letters contain poetic and evocative images of death and rebirth in Christ. In a tract titled *Some Directions to the Panting Soul* (1661), Penington guides discouraged Seekers toward the life for which they so desperately hunger. He employs images of spiritual nourishment that fit well with Jesus' words in this conversation. Just as the Israelites in the wilderness were not to store up the manna from heaven but collect it each day, Penington presses the "necessity of depending on the Spirit for fresh light and life every day" [Penington (1994), p. 206]. He encourages earnest souls that

in the day of his power thou wilt find strength to walk with him; yea, in the day of thy weakness his grace will be sufficient for thee; and he will nurture thee up in his life by his pure Spirit, causing thee to grow under his shadow; and he will be teaching thee to live, and to speak, and to move and act from the principle, and within the compass of his light and life eternal. Only be wise not to catch the notion of things into the earthly part, where the moth can corrupt, and where the thief can break through and steal; but know the divine treasury, where all the things of life are treasured up by the Spirit, and handed forth to the living child with fresh life, according to its need of them. And thus thy heart being kept close to God, and thy spiritual senses continually exercised about the things of God, it will be easy to thee to know the shepherd's voice, and to distinguish the sound of the Spirit in thine own heart. . . . And thus thy life, thy growth, thy path will be sweet, safe, clear, certain, demonstrative in the Spirit and past all reasonings of flesh and blood, either in thyself or others. The beginning of life eternal is in a higher principle than man can come at. Man's wisdom and knowledge of the things of God is but brutish before it [Penington (1994), p. 209].

We can hear echoes here of Jesus' words to Nicodemus about the spiritual birth as a different order of being, unknowable by the earthly mind. Once one learns to wait for and feed upon the daily portion of the Spirit's teaching, one discovers the sufficiency and faithfulness of God. But to store up the bread of life in the intellect, thinking to use it another day as one sees fit, only corrupts it. Penington was by no means anti-intellectual. Educated at Cambridge and a noted spiritual writer before becoming a Quaker, he struggled mightily to get his considerable intellect out of the way of the new birth. It took time for him to place his mind in proper service to the life of the Spirit. As Jesus says in the present conversation, this is the work we must do for the bread that endures for eternal life. This is what it means to *believe* in the one whom God has sent. Belief is not a verbal formulation but a daily dependence upon God.

As Penington's counsel suggests, true belief simplifies the heart and mind. And that inward simplification leads to—indeed *requires*— an outward simplification of life. The Quaker testimony of plainness/ simplicity is aptly expressed in a 1983 statement by Friends in North Carolina Yearly Meeting (Conservative):

Outwardly, simplicity is shunning superfluities of dress, speech, behavior, and possessions, which tend to obscure our vision of reality. Inwardly, simplicity is spiritual detachment from the things of this world as part of the effort to fulfill the first commandment: to love God with all of the heart and mind and strength.

The testimony of outward simplicity began as a protest against the extravagance and snobbery which marked English society in the

1600s. In whatever forms this protest is maintained today, it must be seen as a testimony against involvement with things that tend to dilute our energies and scatter our thoughts, reducing us to lives of triviality and mediocrity.

Simplicity does not mean drabness or narrowness but is essentially positive, being the capacity for selectivity in one who holds attention on the goal. Thus simplicity is an appreciation of all that is helpful towards living as children of the living God [quoted in Whitmire (2001), pp. 23–24].

In seventeenth-century England, the textile industry was at the center of England's early capitalist development. So clothing was a primary form of conspicuous consumption. Changing fashions in apparel were a particular focus of the Quaker protest against extravagance and snobbery. As we listen to Fox's 1667 counsel to Friends, we may apply it to a variety of twenty-first-century fashions and gadgets:

Friends, Keep out of the vain fashions of the world; let not your eyes, and minds, and spirits run after every fashion (in apparel) . . . for that will lead you from the solid life. . . . Therefore, keep all in the modesty, and plainness, and fervency, and sincerity, and be circumspect; for they that follow these things that the world's spirit invents daily, cannot be solid. . . . Therefore, take heed of the world's vanity, and trust not in the uncertain riches . . . but seek the kingdom of God, and the righteousness thereof, and all other things will follow . . . mind the hidden man of the heart, which is a meek and a quiet spirit, which is of great price with the Lord . . . so that you may be as a city set on a hill, that cannot be hid, and as lights to the world, answering the equal principle in all, that God in all things may be glorified [Fox (1831), 7:300–01].

Note how Fox moves from a critique of consumerism, to extolling the virtue of a modest and plainly lived life, to asserting that the light is an "equal principle in all." Simple living is a living testimony that reaches to the witness of God abiding in all persons equally. The simple life is at one with an egalitarian ethic, a conviction that all humanity is equal in the sight of God. As the contemporary saying goes, we "live simply so that others may simply live." Thus, simplicity is a sacramental act. It is an outward sign that expresses and facilitates the inward life of God's grace as our daily bread. Moreover, as we saw in this conversation, the sacramental life is one with humanitarian concern and action.

As we declutter our daily lives, our hearts are tendered to the suffering of others.

In the twentieth century, Quakers witnessed the horror of two world wars. Their conscientious objection to war heightened their sense of its senseless destruction and rampant brutality. Unable to prevent the wars or participate in them, Quaker pacifists sought ways to be part of the healing. One major Quaker effort was to organize and carry out the feeding of millions of starving men, women, and children in Europe after both wars. Their outstanding humanitarian service inspired the Nobel Prize Committee to award its 1947 Peace Prize to Friends worldwide. The simplification of life, both inwardly and outwardly, continues to inspire Friends to a wide variety of service today.

Guided Conversation

The following is an opportunity to experience Christ as the Bread of Life.

> As with all the meditations in this book, it is important to take time to be quiet. Find a quiet place to sit for twenty to thirty minutes or more. Sit in a comfortable but upright position. Still your body for a few moments. Feel yourself breathing; perhaps notice the pulse somewhere in your body. As you come to a place of quiet, calm awareness say, "Here I am."
>
> Now recall an experience of physical hunger. Perhaps you are hungry right now. Locate in your body that feeling of emptiness and want. Remain a few moments with that sense of hunger. How would you describe the feeling? What word, phrase, or image defines it? Take a moment to find the right expression. Check it against the bodily feeling, to know if it fits.
>
> After you have found the sense and an adequate expression of it, consider: does that physical hunger match your spiritual hunger in some way? Does your description of it fit your spiritual experience as well? What is your spiritual dissatisfaction? Be honest with yourself. You may feel that you should be content. But feel your desire. If your physical sense of hunger does not match with your spiritual hunger, how would you define the spiritual emptiness you feel?
>
> Now invite Christ into this meditation. Ask the Bread of Life to be in you, to feed, nurture, refresh your spirit. Find your own words to invite Christ. Then wait in stillness. Be as still as possible. It may heighten your sense of hunger. But that is the place of receiving.

Receive what comes to you there. It may be a revelation, some hint of Christ's teaching in your heart. Or it may simply be a refreshment of your spirit, a satisfaction at the center of your being. That is Christ's flesh and blood, eternal life revived in time. Take time to give thanks for this wonderful gift in Christ, the Bread of Life.

This meditation may be particularly useful if you are struggling with personal issues about food. It may also prove a helpful exercise if you are dealing with any "consumer" issue. How much is enough? With the deeper satisfaction that comes through the Bread of Life, many 'needs' diminish.

A Man Born Blind

John 9:1–41

Conflict escalates rapidly around Jesus in the episodes following the conversation on the Bread of Life. Jesus is again in Jerusalem, for the Feast of Tabernacles. Temple guards are sent to arrest him. But they are awed by his preaching and fail to take him into custody (John 7:32, 46). Nicodemus speaks on behalf of Jesus but is rebuffed by the chief priests and Pharisees (7:50–52). At the Feast (where torches are carried in a night-time procession), Jesus declares, "I am the light of the world. Whoever follows me will never walk in darkness but will have the light of life" (8:12). His ensuing argument with the temple authorities finds both sides increasingly hostile. Jesus speaks increasingly of his impending death (7:6, 33–34; 8:21–29).

Certainly, all four gospels portray a growing conflict between Jesus and the religious authorities. But some scenes probably reflect later debates about Jesus in the synagogues, between Jewish Christians and their critics. That appears to be the case in John 9. The healing of the blind man is set in this particular place to illustrate Jesus as "the light of the world." (As we saw in Conversation 4, the works of Jesus confirm his witness to himself.) The ensuing debate over the healing illustrates how Jewish Christian faith in Jesus developed both before and after his death. So, whatever *literal* events in Jesus' life are recounted here, John probably combines multiple events and composite characters in the writing of this story. The outcome is a powerful *literary* production that represents faith in Jesus as it formed both during and after his life. But the aim of the story is that we find its truth in our own conversation with Christ.

> **9:1–7:** As he walked along, he saw a man blind from birth. His disciples asked him, "Rabbi, who sinned, this man or his parents, that he was born blind?" Jesus answered, "Neither this man nor his parents sinned; he was born blind so that God's works might be revealed in him. We must work the works of him who sent me while it is day; night

is coming when no man can work. As long as I am in the world, I am the light of the world." When he had said this, he spat on the ground and made mud with the saliva and spread the mud on the man's eyes, saying to him, "Go, wash in the pool of Siloam" (which means Sent). Then he went and washed and came back able to see.

The story begins with Jesus and his disciples walking the streets of Jerusalem, where they see a man blind from birth. The encounter provokes the disciples to engage in a perennial Jewish debate. According to tradition, such a condition must be God's judgment upon sin. But *whose* *sin* is it: the man's parents' sin, or his own sin? To resolve this conundrum, some rabbis taught that those with congenital defects must have sinned in the womb. The question is basically one of *origins*, the *cause* of the man's condition. It is a matter of moral casuistry.

But Jesus rejects the premise altogether. He replies, "He was born blind so that God's works might be revealed in him." Now, one might conclude from his remark that *God caused* this man to be born blind in order that Jesus could come along one day and heal him. But that logic is still mired in the question of origins. Jesus approaches the matter from the opposite direction. He makes no conjecture as to cause here. He simply acknowledges that the man is blind. His concern for the man's present condition focuses not on its origins but its *purpose* and *destiny*. It's not about the past but the future. Rather than view the man as the outcome of a flawed past, Jesus discovers in him an *opportunity* to reveal God's power. Hence, Jesus interrupts the standard human concern with cause and effect, to suggest a radically different, redemptive future. Further, he emphasizes the timeliness of this moment: "We must work the works of him who sent me while it is day; night is coming when no one can work." There is note of urgency here: he knows his time is growing short.

The actual healing of the man is described briefly, because the ensuing controversy is John's main concern in this story. Like the feeding of the five thousand in the preceding conversation, this man's healing is a good thing in itself. But as it redirects his life, the story really takes off.

9:8-12: The neighbors and those who had seen him before as a beggar began to ask, "Is this not the man who used to sit and beg?" Some were saying, "It is he." Others were saying, "No, but it is someone like him."

He kept saying, "I am the man." But they kept asking him, "Then how were your eyes opened?" He answered, "The man called Jesus made mud, spread it on my eyes, and said to me, 'Go to Siloam and wash,' Then I went and washed and received my sight." They said to him, "Where is he?" He said, "I do not know."

The controversy begins with the man's neighbors. No one seems to know him well. They cannot decide if this is the same man they formerly knew to be a blind beggar. Verbs of continuing action here suggest protracted confusion. The healed man keeps insisting that he is the same man they formerly knew. He recounts in detail the story of his healing. He has gained physical sight, but he has no particular view regarding his healer. He simply refers to "the man called Jesus." Moreover, he has no idea where Jesus now is.

9:13–23: They brought to the Pharisees the man who had formerly been blind. Now it was a Sabbath day when Jesus made the mud and opened his eyes. Then the Pharisees also began to ask him how he had received his sight. He said to them, "He put mud on my eyes. Then I washed, and now I see." Some of the Pharisees said, "This man is not from God, for he does not observe the Sabbath." But others said, "How can a man who is a sinner perform such signs?" And they were divided. So they said again to the blind man, "What do you say about him? It was your eyes he opened." He said, "He is a prophet."

The Jews did not believe that he had been blind and had received his sight until they called the parents of the man who had received his sight and asked them, "Is this your son, who you say was born blind? How then does he now see?" His parents answered, "We know that this is our son, and that he was born blind; but we do not know how it is that he now sees, nor do we know who opened his eyes. Ask him; he is of age. He will speak for himself." His parents said this because they were afraid of the Jews; for the Jews had already agreed that anyone who confessed Jesus to be the Messiah would be put out of the synagogue. Therefore his parents said, "He is of age; ask him."

We now learn that the healing took place on the Sabbath. This detail brings the "moral police" into the story. The Pharisees ask the man *how* he received his sight. He gives the sequence of events, describing the *technique* Jesus apparently used in healing him. Questions of technique, of course, are all about cause and effect. But the Pharisees are less concerned with details of technique than with inappropriate timing. How could a man of God heal on the Sabbath? (John may be satirizing the teaching of the Pharisees here: spitting in the dust would amount to working on the Sabbath?) On the other hand, others argue that he could not do such things if he were not from God. As he listens to their debate, however, the healed man begins to have a view about Jesus. When they ask him his opinion, he answers that Jesus is a prophet. Physical sight is leading on towards spiritual sight: *he's starting to see Jesus.*

Hearing his answer, the Pharisees grow suspicious. Might this man be a shill, working with Jesus to trick the gullible? So they question his parents (his progenitors—his *cause*) to confirm that this man is their son, to ask whether he was indeed born blind, and if they know why he now sees. The parents are unsure what their son has gotten himself into. They are afraid to tangle with religious authority, so they reply coyly, "He is of age; ask him." (And leave us out of it!) John's explanation that to confess Jesus could mean expulsion from the synagogue is anachronistic. Such disciplinary action against Jewish Christians began only decades later.

> **9:24-34:** So for the second time they called the man who had been blind, and they said to him, "Give glory to God! We know that this man is a sinner." He answered, "I do not know whether he is a sinner. One thing I do know, that though I was blind, now I see." They said to him, "What did he do to you? How did he open your eyes?" He answered them, "I have told you already and you would not listen. Why do you want to hear it again? Do you also want to become his disciples?" Then they reviled him, saying, "You are his disciple, but we are disciples of Moses. We know that God has spoken to Moses, but as for this man, we do not know where he comes from." The man answered, "Here is an astonishing thing! You do not know where he comes from, and yet he opened my eyes. We know that God does not listen to sinners, but he does listen to one who worships him and obeys his will. Never since the world began has it been heard that anyone opened the eyes of a person born blind. If this man were not from God, he could do nothing." They answered him, "You were born entirely in sins, and are you trying to teach us?" And they drove him out.

Note how much of the conversation in this story is *about* Jesus, *without* him. As such, it becomes increasingly combative. Literarily, this may be the most entertaining conversation in the Gospel of John! The healed man begins to tease the Pharisees and side with Jesus openly, even truculently. Again, the question of origins preoccupies the Pharisees. They complain that they don't know where this Jesus comes from. The controversy makes them *obdurately blind* to the miracle before them, even as it drives the healed man passionately towards *true vision*. While others speculate and make judgments, he sticks to his story; he remains grounded in his own experience. That becomes his path to true faith.

If we view these arguments as reflecting synagogue controversies in the decades after Jesus' death, we glimpse how the Christian controversy polarized the Jewish community. It drove some to revile Jesus and his followers as impious troublemakers. It inspired others to believe in Jesus and defend his followers. Their theological claims for Jesus escalated, even at the risk of excommunication, expulsion from the community ("They drove him out").

> **9:35–41:** Jesus heard that they had driven him out, and when he found him, he said, "Do you believe in the Son of Man?" He answered, "And who is he, sir? Tell me, so that I may believe in him." Jesus said to him, "You have seen him, and the one speaking to you is he." He said, "Lord, I believe." And he worshiped him. Jesus said, "I came into this world for judgment so that those who do not see may see, and those who see may become blind." Some of the Pharisees near him heard this and said to him, "Surely we are not blind, are we?" Jesus said to them, "If you were blind, you would not have sin. But now that you say, 'We see,' your sin remains."

Again, official excommunication would have been unlikely during Jesus' lifetime. It is worth noting that when excommunication did occur, it was not exclusion in the narrowly religious sense we would imagine today. It was a general social ban. When early Jewish Christians faced excommunication, they found themselves in religious, social, and economic difficulty. But that difficulty also drove them more strongly into solidarity with one another and into Christian faith.

Hearing of his expulsion, Jesus tracks down the man, now a pariah in his own neighborhood. At this point, he still sees Jesus only as a healer and a prophet. He responds blankly to Jesus' question regarding the Son of Man. Perhaps he is not even familiar with that particular title and form of messianic expectation. Jesus explains, "You have seen him, and the one speaking to you is he." New spiritual sight is like new physical sight: you see, but you may not know *what* you see. Once the identification is made, however, the man believes and abjectly worships Jesus. His healing into sight is now complete. He is an excommunicated Jew in Jerusalem; but he lives that identity with a new freedom. His life has been turned from a past-present to a future-present.

Jesus' words about sight and judgment echo his remarks to Nicodemus (Conversation 2). Judgment is the light of truth coming into the world. People believe by turning to the light, living its truth. To turn away is to choose blindness. Jesus can heal our blindness, our obtuseness to the truth. But when we insist that our blindness is sight, then we resist healing, we resist life itself. As the light of the world, Jesus is a healer. But his healing is also judgment. The way we respond to the light enacts the judgment in our lives.

Writing in the midst of these increasingly dire controversies, John is relentlessly negative in his portrayal of the Pharisees and other religious leaders who eventually handed Jesus over to the Romans. Christian readers tend to accept his portrayal of the Pharisees uncritically. But what would have happened to this man without their interrogations? Until they blundered upon the scene, we have no indication that physical sight had transformed him spiritually. The eventual parting of ways between Jews and Christians is a painful story. Yet, through that parting, two great Abrahamic faiths emerged into their own true vocations. Jews continue to count Abraham as the great origin of their people and their faith. Christians, however, exist in a paradoxical relation to Abraham. We find our lineage in him only through our rebirth in Christ, who said, "Before Abraham was, I am" (8:58). That utterance nearly got him stoned right on the spot (8:59)! It also immediately precedes our present conversation. It introduces a rupture, *an apocalyptic undoing of time*, whereby eternity invades time, destiny redefines origins, a future cause produces present effects, and the future-present explodes the categories of the past-present.

Reflections from the Quaker Tradition

The early Quaker movement understood itself as a revolution in human consciousness. But it was not simply a private revolution. As early

Friends turned to the light of Christ in their consciences, they saw themselves and their society with new eyes. The light also led them to experiment with new patterns of personal and social behavior. These "testimonies" (introduced in our previous conversations) demonstrated a more egalitarian, peaceful and just society. The Quaker movement therefore offended and threatened ruling classes in the clerical, economic, and political realms of seventeenth-century England. The movement was persecuted as soon as it became visible.

The persecutions of early Friends created occasions for a great deal of political drama, especially courtroom drama. Quaker leaders were brought to trial for their controversial message. Whole meetings were arrested and brought before judges just for gathering to worship. Although Friends often suffered imprisonment and fines for their faith, they saw their courtroom appearances as moments of truth that could alter the consciousness of many around them. Indeed, the capricious and cruel miscarriages of law against Friends disturbed the consciences of many tender people in the community. Some notable instances can be mentioned here.

James Nayler was a dropout from Parliament's army in the English Civil War when he joined the Quaker movement. He became an extraordinary preacher and leader. He was tried for blasphemy in Westmorland in 1653. His defense in court was so compelling that the judge, Anthony Pearson, was convinced over the course of the trial and himself became a Quaker. Nayler went on to become the most incendiary leader of the movement's first decade. His preaching and debating in London drew large crowds, which included many people of influence. In 1656, he and a group of followers came to Bristol and enacted Christ's entry into Jerusalem. They meant it to symbolize Christ's coming in common people like themselves. Nayler played the role of Jesus.

Parliament seized upon the incident as an opportunity to stigmatize Nayler and the entire Quaker movement. A long, elaborate show-trial ensued, on the largest possible political stage, before Parliament itself. Despite the fact that Nayler clearly stated he didn't claim to be Christ, he was condemned as a messianic pretender and barbarously punished. One of Nayler's followers, Mary Booth, wrote of the trial in terms similar to those Jesus uses in condemning the blindness of the Pharisees. She describes Nayler as

A follower of the Lamb in many Tribulations, where-ever he went [see Revelation 14:1–5], who was baptized into his death by the Holy Ghost, and by Fire; made like unto him through sufferings. . . . He was set as a Sign for the Rise and Fall of many, that the Secrets of many hearts might be made manifest [see Luke 2:34–35], and to prove [that is, "test"] that Generation that then had power in their hands, but improved it not, but went on in the Counsel of their own corrupt Hearts to persecute the Innocent [quoted in Gwyn (1995), p. 175].

Thus, Booth interpreted Nayler's trial as a moment of truth for the English Commonwealth. Parliament's unjust punishment of Nayler steered that regime toward eventual collapse. Early Christians similarly understood the fall of Jerusalem forty years after the trial and crucifixion of Jesus to be the inevitable outcome of the failure of the chief priests, scribes, and Pharisees in their moment of truth.

The Restoration of monarchy and state Church in England in 1660 only worsened the persecutions of early Friends, however. Quakers were the most notorious social radicals and stubborn resisters of the state-enforced Church. They came in for savage treatment from a government bent on returning to the arrangements of an earlier time. The courtroom appearances of arrested Quaker leaders continued to provide high drama. For example, during a year spent imprisoned at Lancaster Castle, Fox's sensational appearances at quarterly Assize sessions created enough local unrest that authorities finally transferred him across the North to Scarborough Castle.

One Quaker trial produced a landmark decision that altered the practice of English court law. In 1670 William Penn and William Meade were arrested at a banned Quaker gathering in London. Penn was the most highborn convert to the Quaker movement. He was especially controversial owing to his social rank. Penn had been educated in law and made a compelling defense. He argued that laws against Quakers were contrary to the fundamental laws of England. The Lord Mayor of London sat as presiding judge for this important trial. It was the custom of the day for the judge to direct the jury in their decision. The Lord Mayor instructed the jury to return a guilty verdict. But the jury refused and found Penn and Meade innocent. After considerable browbeating from the judge and intimidation from the court recorder, the jury was sequestered without food or drink to reconsider its verdict.

When the jury reappeared two days later, it still refused the judge. The jury was then fined and imprisoned for the next two months. Finally, a full assembly of judges was convened and established the right of juries to their own judgments.

Certainly, the legal travesties of the Penn-Meade trial astonish us today. The records of early Quaker trials are full of such tactics by authorities desperate to suppress a group of Christian pacifists. But the precedent set by the Penn-Meade trial not only established the legal right to be judged by one's peers. It also created the legal space for God's light (or human reason, if you prefer) to move and advance in human society, untrammeled by the dictates of ruling interests. The trial was one skirmish in a larger struggle in which early Friends played an important role in the establishment of religious freedom. Their pacifist resistance under persecution also helped advance the democratic concept of a loyal opposition in politics. And, as noted in Conversation 1, the Quaker one-price system in trade helped reduce deceptive practices in the marketplace. All these and more social changes become possible when men and women take seriously the light's rightful place at the center of human conscience (see Matt. 5:15–16).

Guided Conversation

As with all the meditations in this book, it is important to take time to be quiet. Find a quiet place to sit for twenty to thirty minutes or more. Sit in a comfortable but upright position. Still your body for a few moments. Feel yourself breathing; perhaps notice the pulse somewhere in your body. As you come to a place of quiet, calm awareness say, "Here I am."

Now take a few moments to consider what is happening in your life. Focus on a matter causing your some anxiety, difficulty, or dissatisfaction. After you have chosen one situation, review your understanding of it. What is your responsibility for it? What is the responsibility of others? Do you feel that God is causing this to happen? Or is God simply allowing it? Take a moment to review your understanding of the difficulty as it presently stands.

Now step back from analysis. Ask yourself how this difficulty feels. Sit quietly with the question. Your stillness will help ground the question in your body and bring an answer to your awareness. After you have found that feeling, continue sitting quietly with it. Don't immerse yourself in it.

Don't go into turbulence. Just sit quietly near it. Is there a word or phrase that describes it?

Now sense Christ with you. Visualize Christ with you, if you wish. How do you sense Christ in relation to this difficulty? If you are visualizing Christ, you may see Christ in some spatial relationship to you or to others. Or you may simply sense Christ present with you. What word or phrase would you give to Christ's presence in this situation? Take a moment to test the word or phrase, to feel if it really fits what you sense.

Now, your sense of Christ in the situation with you—does it suggest a path of action to take? Christ may be leading you to take action. But be careful. You may want to give this possible leading time before acting on it. You may wish to check it with someone whose judgment you trust. Or there may be no clear sense of direction coming from this meditation. Your sense of Christ with you may be simply an encouraging and uphold-ing presence. There may be no particular action for you to take just now. This may be a time of waiting.

Whatever you glean from this meditation, take a moment in closing to be thankful for whatever peace or insight you have received. Ask for guidance, patience, and strength to endure and overcome this difficulty. Ask in confidence of God's good will for you, and for others involved in this situation—including any adversaries. God will not lead you to hurt anyone, including yourself.

You may wish to reflect later on this meditation. If you feel you received help from Christ, what relation does that gift have to your earlier analyses of your dilemma? Often, what comes through the meditation comes at a different level or from a different direction. It may take you in an unexpected direction. That doesn't mean that your cause-and-effect analyses of the situation were wrong or worthless. But it should remind you that analysis has its limits. Unchecked, it may blind you to what Christ is doing in your life.

The Gate, the Good Shepherd
John 10:1–21

A s we continue to "listen in" on conversations between Jesus and various individuals and groups, we begin to hear something of Christ speaking to us today. A subtle shift occurs: listening to the words of these ancient stories, a voice speaks *through* and *beyond* them. It is a listening equivalent of looking at an object before you. At first, you look closely at the object. Then, as you allow your gaze to soften, you begin looking through and beyond it. In the process, the object becomes less a "thing" to scrutinize and more part of a larger reality. The language of John's gospel has a similar effect. It is important to focus intently, listen carefully to the words. But at a certain point, the symbols, ironies, and paradoxes overwhelm the mind, and one's focus shifts to an indeterminate point beyond them. That is where Christ awaits, to begin the conversation in earnest.

The present conversation extends the controversy between Jesus and the religious leaders who denounced his healing of the blind man. Jesus takes the controversy to the next level. But he is not satisfied simply to exacerbate division and stalemate. He enunciates the new unity and direction his followers are finding with him. All the conversations up to this point have focused mainly upon the individual's relationship to Christ. This conversation turns decisively towards the Christian community forming around Jesus, forming in Christ. Subsequent conversations will advance in that same direction, as Jesus prepares his followers to continue without his physical presence.

> **10:1–21:** "Very truly, I tell you, anyone who does not enter the sheepfold by the gate but climbs in by another way is a thief and a bandit. The one who enters by the gate is the shepherd of the sheep. The gatekeeper opens the gate for him, and the sheep hear his voice. He calls his own sheep by name and leads them out. When he has brought out all his own, he goes ahead of them, and the sheep follow him because

they know his voice. They will not follow a stranger, but they run from him because they do not know the voice of strangers." Jesus used this figure of speech with them, but they did not understand what he was saying to them.

So again Jesus said to them, "Very truly, I tell you, I am the gate for the sheep. All who came before me are thieves and bandits, but the sheep did not listen to them. I am the gate. Whoever enters by me will be saved, and will come in and go out and find pasture. The thief comes only to steal and destroy. I came that they may have life, and have it abundantly.

"I am the good shepherd. The good shepherd lays down his life for the sheep. The hired hand, who is not the shepherd and does not own the sheep, sees the wolf coming and leaves the sheep and runs away— and the wolf snatches them and scatters them. The hired hand runs away because a hired hand does not care for the sheep. I am the good shepherd. I know my own and my own know me, just as the Father knows me and I know the Father. And I lay down my life for the sheep. I have other sheep that do not belong to this fold. I must bring them also, and they will listen to my voice. So there will be one flock, one shepherd. For this reason the Father loves me, because I lay down my life in order to take it up again. No one takes it from me, but I lay it down of my own accord. I have power to lay it down, and I have power to take it up again. I have received this command from my Father."

Again the Jews were divided because of these words. Many of them were saying, "He has a demon and is out of his mind. Why listen to him?" Others were saying, "These are not the words of one who has a demon. Can a demon open the eyes of the blind?"

After commenting on the blindness of the Pharisees around him (the end of Chapter 9), Jesus suddenly reflects on sheep and shepherding. Once again, his hearers are lost! Apparently, they do not voice their confusion, but Jesus senses it and then speaks more plainly. His two annunciations, "I am the gate" and "I am the good shepherd," are intimately related. It seems strange to us that Jesus would describe himself as both the gate and the shepherd. But it would have made sense to his hearers. Traditional sheepfolds are still seen in Palestine. They are simple, circular stone walls, with a gap allowing the passage of sheep in and out. Even today, shepherds still lie across the gap at night to keep the sheep in and intruders out. So the shepherd *is* the gate.

In saying "I am the gate for the sheep," Jesus identifies himself as the *threshold* of salvation, the portal to eternal, abundant life. The sheepfold is not for a single sheep, but for a flock of sheep, a community. Jesus clearly has the Pharisees and other religious authorities in mind when he speaks of thieves and bandits raiding the flock. These do not enter by the gate, the true way that Jesus opens. Moreover, they speak in a voice the sheep do not recognize and will flee. Jesus clearly implies that religious leaders have not spoken with an authority most people recognize or will follow. His bandit imagery even suggests that they prey upon their own people.

In saying "I am the good shepherd," Jesus identifies himself as the *true leader* of his people. They are not simply on their own as they pass through the gate, but they follow his voice to good pasture, to abundant life. But the decisive quality of his leadership is this: *he lays down his life for his people.* Jesus clearly anticipates his death. But the present tense of his wording suggests that the voice of the eternal Christ speaks through the words of Jesus.

The image of the shepherd was powerful in Hebrew Scripture long before Jesus. The pastoral ideal was strongly fixed in the culture and spirituality of the people. Abraham, Isaac, Jacob, Rachel, Moses, Zipporah, and David were all shepherds at least part of their lives. David composed his greatest Psalm based upon his experience as a shepherd. Most pointedly, Jesus echoes here the oracle of Ezekiel (Chapter 34), in which the Lord chastises the leaders of Israel as bad shepherds who neglect, scatter, and prey upon the flock. God promises to become the shepherd of the flock, through God's servant David (that is, a descendent of that royal line).

David risked his life defending his flock against lions and bears (1 Sam. 17:34-35). Jesus enlarges upon this aspect and makes it the key to his identity as the good, true shepherd. He contrasts himself with the "hired hand," who runs when the wolf approaches. The hired shepherd works under some form of limited *contract* which does not require self-sacrifice. But Jesus defines his role in *covenantal* terms, a relationship of deeper intimacy and unlimited commitment. "I am the good shepherd, I know my own and my own know me, just as the Father knows me and I know the Father." This is the first instance of imagery Jesus will use several times in his parting conversation with his disciples. As initiator of a new covenant, Jesus mediates between his followers and the Father. On both sides, the relationship is based upon intimacy and love, not distance and fear. But this covenant will be sealed with his own blood.

Jesus' hearers would have known better than most of us today what obtuse, digressive creatures sheep can be. The shepherd works diligently to keep the flock together. This is not a flattering image of the human condition! But the conversations in John's gospel repeatedly portray just how obtuse we humans can be on the spiritual level. Even Nicodemus, a respected teacher of the people, is confused by Jesus' teaching. The health and safety of the sheep consist in staying together with one another and with the shepherd. So the pastoral image fits well with the spiritual needs of humans, even the best and brightest. The safety of the flock lies in the ability of the sheep to *follow together* the voice of the shepherd.

If you observe sheep, you notice that they follow one another as much as they follow their shepherd's voice. Their attention is focused downward as they search for food. So they generally move with the others around them—unless some particularly tasty-looking plant draws them in another direction. Human social and congregational dynamics are not so different. We are more often drawn by the example or advice of others than by the voice of the Good Shepherd. Hence, each member relies upon, and must contribute to, the healthy dynamic and direction of the congregation. Each must listen diligently for the voice of Christ, both for one's own sake and for one's part in the community of faith. That is the reality of a covenantal faith.

In this conversation, using images of the gate and the good shepherd, Jesus presents himself as the means of salvation. He is both *threshold* and *guide* to the sheep. Yet *our means* is *his end*, in two senses. First, it is the *end of his life* as he lays it down for the sheep. Second, it is also the *aim of his ministry*. Thus, Jesus adds emphatically that no one takes his life from him, but he lays it down in order to take it up again. It is his aim to do so. In the Gospel of John, Jesus speaks symbolically, theologically, from the *ex post facto* perspective of the resurrection. The human pathos of his rejection, suffering and death are almost entirely eclipsed. Indeed, in John, the voice of the risen Christ nearly replaces that of the earthly Jesus. Some statements by the narrator and by Jesus may sound highly dogmatic by themselves, but are intended paradoxically and mystically. That reality emerges when we engage with the conversations in terms of experience, rather than doctrine. (We will return to this feature in John in the Conclusion to this book.)

As Jesus looks toward his death and the community of followers that will survive him, he alludes to other sheep "not of this fold," who will listen to his voice and follow him. "So there will be one flock, one shepherd." He may refer to the Gentile mission that will develop soon after his death. The conversation with the Samaritan woman (see Conversation 3) has already placed that epochal development on the horizon. The union of Jew and Gentile in Christ will be accomplished through Jesus' death and the voice of the good shepherd calling both together to himself, to a worship in spirit and truth (John 4:24). Again, *his end is our means.* Our encounter with the crucified and risen Lord breaks through and transforms us. That encounter, and the spiritual practice that keeps us coming back to it, are the means, or mode, the threshold through which we encounter one another in spirit and truth. It creates and maintains us as one flock, under one shepherd.

This conversation ends as a conversation among "the Jews" who have been listening to these exalted words of Jesus. Again, they are divided in their impressions. But the most important point is that the conversation between them and Jesus has broken down. They have withdrawn, to talk *about* Jesus rather than *with* him. That turn will accelerate the process leading to his arrest and relinquishment to Rome.

Reflections from the Quaker Tradition

The Quaker movement gathered with a resolute desire to be led directly by Christ, the one true shepherd. And since the same Christ speaks in the conscience of each individual, they expected to find unity. So Fox wrote in 1652 "To the flock of God about Sedburgh. Every one in your measure wait upon God, who is the true shepherd, and leads his flock to green pastures, and fresh springs he opens daily; this ye will see and experience. And mind that which is pure in one another, which joins you together; for nothing will join, or make fit, but what is pure" [Fox (1831), 7:21]. In a 1669 epistle, Fox wrote, "All that are gathered in the name of Jesus, and are made alive by him and quickened by him, come to the flock of Christ; and know where they feed at noon-day . . . the bread of life and water of life are not only given to feed yourselves, but by them you may feed others, and refresh others" [Fox (1831), 8:15]. So the one true shepherd not only leads the flock and nourishes them, but they nourish one another with what they receive from the shepherd.

The movement renounced professional leadership. They viewed academic training as irrelevant at best to preaching by the Spirit's leading. At worst, it entraps one in an intellectual or "notional" impression of faith. Once again their perspective was particularly informed by the situation at the end of the Reformation. They saw how competing and warring churches had been led and misled time and again by their "hireling" shepherds. In a tract *To All Sorts of People in Christendom* (1667), Fox wrote,

> There is but one shepherd, and one fold, and the sheep know the shepherd's voice, and follow him . . . he died for them, and hath purchased them with his blood: and therefore, they are not their own, but Christ's. . . . But in the world there is a multitude of shepherds, and they have their several flocks and folds; and the shepherds fall out with themselves, and with their flocks . . . and one while, one shepherd getteth the flock, and another while, another shepherd getteth the flock, and by these doings the flocks are almost plucked to pieces. . . . And you may see as many flocks as there are in the world, there are so many shepherds knowing of them, and keeping them in the world, which the devil hath made a wilderness [Fox (1831), 4:326–27].

This is an uncharitable view, to be sure (although one can still find it borne out today). But again, Fox and early Friends understood the criticisms Jesus made against the Scribes and Pharisees to be applicable to the Church establishment of their day. And these criticisms were often justified. In particular, rural parts of England, where the Quaker movement began, had long been neglected by the national parish system, which often sent the least gifted and most corruptible men to serve parishes.

A century later, John Woolman was a non-professional Quaker minister in colonial New Jersey. His remarkable *Journal* has made him a beloved example to Friends and others since his death in 1771. In his early twenties, he began to sense a gift in ministry. He attended Quaker meetings for worship "in an awful frame of mind and endeavoured to be inwardly acquainted with the language of the True Shepherd" [Woolman (1971), p. 31]. Mary Rose O'Reilley compares tuning into that voice to the practice of music student, listening to a tuning fork first thing every morning. Over time and with patient attention, one gradually becomes attuned to the frequency of A440 [Heller (2003), p. 140]. The voice of the shepherd becomes the source to which one can—and must—regularly return.

One of Woolman's most celebrated undertakings was to persuade American Friends to free their slaves. This involved a great deal of visitation and gentle counsel among Quaker slave owners. Woolman found these encounters difficult. On traveling in Maryland in 1757, he reflected, "As the people in this and the southern provinces live much on the labour of slaves, many of whom are used hardly, my concern was that I might attend with singleness of heart to the voice of the True Shepherd and be so supported as to remain unmoved at the faces of men" [Woolman (1971), p. 59]. Woolman's personality was not strident. He found it difficult to confront people with their misdeeds. But in Christ, who laid down his life for his sheep, he found courage to speak the truth in love.

From the beginning of the Quaker movement, Friends believed that Christ's voice speaks through all consciences. That implies that Christ may be known and followed by people beyond the bounds of Christian culture and belief. During his brief sojourn in America, Fox's conversations with African slaves and Native Americans convinced him that many knew the voice of the shepherd. These may be understood as the "other sheep that do not belong to this fold" whom Jesus mentions. In 1761, John Woolman was moved to visit a group of Delaware Indians in Wyalusing, about two hundred miles from Philadelphia. He writes that he had for many years

> felt love in my heart toward the natives of this land who dwell far back in the wilderness, whose ancestors were owners and possessors of the land where we dwell, and who for a very small consideration assigned their inheritance to us. . . . And in conversation with them by an interpreter, as also by observations on their countenance and conduct, I believed some of them were measurably acquainted with that divine power which subjects the rough and forward will of the creature; and at times I felt inward drawings toward a visit to that place [pp. 122–23].

Finally, in 1763, Woolman and a companion made the trip, which required passing through areas where fighting between Indians and white settlers had broken out. Woolman was acutely aware of the danger but continued to feel divine love drawing him on. He went, hoping that "I might feel and understand their life and the spirit they live in, if haply I might receive some instruction from them, or they be in any degree helped forward by my following the leadings of Truth amongst them" [p. 127]. So clearly, he was ready to hear as well as speak. Finally, he reached Wyalusing and had meetings with the Indians and a friendly Moravian missionary. Woolman describes one meeting in which he tried to speak to the group through interpreters. But the interpreters didn't share enough English and Delaware among them to proceed very helpfully. Finally,

> I told the interpreters that I found it in my heart to pray to God and believed if I prayed right he would hear me, and expressed my willingness for them to omit interpreting; so our meeting ended with a degree of divine love. And before the people went out I observed Papunehang (the man who had been zealous in labouring for a reformation in that town, being then very tender) spoke to one of the interpreters, and I was afterward told that he said in substance as follows: "I love to feel where words come from" [p. 133].

Here was another soul acquainted with the voice of the true shepherd.

Guided Conversation

Fox writes of Christ as "the door into the holy way, for his holy people to walk in.... And this never came out of the brain-beaten stuff of man, nor of his chamber of imagery [see Ezek. 8:12]" [Fox (1831), 8:43]. In other words, the door doesn't open to us through our mental efforts. The following is an opportunity to experience Christ as that door, or gate, a threshold to new life. Just as sheep often balk at passing through the gate to the sheepfold, we may balk at the gate Christ opens to us. This exercise focuses on making that passage together with others.

As with all the meditations in this book, it is important to take time to be quiet. Find a quiet place to sit for twenty to thirty minutes or more. Sit in a comfortable but upright position. Still your body for a few moments.

Feel yourself breathing; perhaps notice the pulse somewhere in your body. As you come to a place of quiet, calm awareness say, "Here I am."

Now take a few moments to consider what is happening in your life. Focus on a decision or transition you face with one or more other persons close to you. It might be a spouse or family member, or members of your congregation. Take a moment to get in touch with the uncertainty or anxiety you feel about that decision or transition. Does it also involve fear, resentment, anger, confusion, impatience with the others? Identify the feelings. Locate them in your body, and stay with that sense for a moment. Just witness it—don't become entangled in it.

Now, listen for a voice calling your name. Or imagine a voice calling your name. Is it a familiar voice? It may be the voice of someone in your life. Is it a reassuring voice? If not, disregard it and wait to hear a more familiar, reassuring voice. When you have heard that voice, wait to hear if it has something to tell you about your dilemma. Wait with expectation or openness, Christ may use that voice to say something about your dilemma and how to move through it.

If nothing happens, that's OK. Over the next hours or days, you still may sense something shift in your attitude toward the matter and the others involved. It may be a sense of reassurance about making that passage together. It may give a sense of guidance, about what to do or say. Whether it comes immediately or later, if you receive something helpful, give thanks to God. You may want to ask God for the clarity and courage to act accordingly. Spend a few more moments in quiet stillness with the Lord.

You may wish to share the guidance you have received with others involved with you in the decision or transition. Or with someone else whose judgment you trust. That person may help you discern if this is a true leading. You could share it with your pastor or priest. He or she is only a "hired hand," but may help you discern the voice of the good shepherd and God's will for your life.

CONVERSATION 8

The Father

John 12:20–36

The raising of Lazarus (John 11) is the final and most provocative sign of Jesus' ministry. It reveals him to be "the resurrection and the life" (11:25) and precipitates decisive action from the governing council of chief priests and scribes. Besides the theological scandal of Jesus' claims, they fear that rising popular acclaim and expectation will result in social upheaval and a Roman crackdown. The temple could be destroyed and the nation devolve to direct Roman rule.

As the collaborationist regime in Judea, the council cannot allow that to happen. The high priest, Caiaphas, epitomizes the case for a preemptive response to Jesus: "It is better for you to have one man die for the people than to have the whole nation destroyed" (11:50). Once again in John, human wisdom and strategy play naïvely into God's larger purposes. John makes the irony explicit by adding, "He did not say this on his own, but being high priest that year he prophesied that Jesus was about to die for the nation, and not for the nation only, but to gather into one the dispersed children of God. So from that day on they planned to put him to death" (11:51–53).

A week later, as the Passover begins, Jesus makes a sensational public entry into Jerusalem. The crowd hails him as their king. These developments only confirm the council's worst fears. They are losing control of the city. They say among themselves, "You see, you can do nothing. Look, the world has gone after him!" (12:19).

12:20–33: Now among those who went up to worship at the festival were some Greeks. They came to Philip, who was from Bethsaida in Galilee, and said to him, "Sir, we wish to see Jesus." Philip went and told Andrew; then Andrew and Philip went and told Jesus. Jesus answered them, "The hour has come for the Son of Man to be glorified. Very truly, I tell you, unless a grain of wheat falls into the earth and dies, it remains just a single grain; but if it dies, it bears much fruit.

Those who love their life lose it, and those who hate their life in this world will keep it for eternal life. Whoever serves me must follow me, and where I am, there will my servant be also. Whoever serves me, the Father will honor.

"Now my soul is troubled. And what should I say—'Father, save me from this hour'? No, it is for this reason that I have come to this hour. Father, glorify your name." Then a voice came from heaven, "I have glorified it, and I will glorify it again." The crowd standing there heard it and said that it was thunder. Others said, "An angel has spoken to him." Jesus answered, "This voice has come for your sake, not for mine. Now is the judgment of this world; now the ruler of this world will be driven out. And I, when I am lifted up from the earth, will draw all people to myself." He said this to indicate the kind of death he was to die.

"The world" going after Jesus is more than the Judean world. Now "Greeks" are seeking him. The term is ambiguous. It may mean Diaspora Jews, more assimilated to Greek culture than Judeans, but in town for the festival. Or it may suggest Greek-speaking Gentiles generally, rather than ethnic Greeks as such. As we saw earlier, regarding "the Jews," such designations in the ancient world usually referred to religious or cultural orientation, rather than ethnicity as such. From a Palestinian Jewish perspective, the "Greeks" would signify the rest of the "world," since Greek culture and language dominated the Eastern Mediterranean.

There are no parallels to this passage in the other three gospels. And there is no indication here that Jesus actually met these "Greeks." In a manner typical of John's gospel, this development serves theological and *ex post facto* perspectives. The arrival of "Greeks" (Jewish or Gentile) upon the horizon signals events to come after Jesus' death. So Jesus interprets their inquiry as the sign that his hour has come. Yet, Jesus speaks of the Son of Man in the third person singular (as he usually does in all four gospels). There is no doubt that we are to identify Jesus with the Son of Man. But as noted in Conversation 1, this ambiguous term can also connote humans generally. Hence, a paradox: the arrival of Greeks seeking Jesus signals the *universal significance* of the *unique person* of Jesus Christ. The two senses of "Son of Man" converge at this decisive hour.

The manner in which this Son of Man will be "glorified," to the universal benefit of humankind, is also paradoxical. "Very truly," Jesus begins (the Greek text here preserves the Aramaic *Amen Amen*, an emphatic affirmation). The ensuing parable of the seed falling to the ground states the case succinctly: Christ remains unique, "single," God's "only Son" (3:16), unless he dies. But as he dies, he bears his true fruit. The universal Son of Man is raised up in all. This parallels the affirmation in John's Prologue, that the light and life of God is in everyone, but is revealed by the unique incarnation of the light in Jesus Christ.

Jesus then enunciates the paradoxical axiom that appears in all four gospels: to lose one's life is to gain it; to love one's life is to lose it. In John, Jesus states that "those who hate their life in this world will keep it for eternal life." This adds an element that fits with his other statements about "the world." To hate one's life in this world is to disown one's life as the world defines it, renounce the socially constructed self, and allow God to define and destine one's life. Jesus will reveal that destiny in his death. The Son of Man will be glorified. *Glory* is the *unworldly beauty and holiness of God*. At his impending hour, Jesus' identification with the Father will be complete. He promises that whoever follows him in this path will be his true servant, honored by the Father.

This is an excruciating paradox. Even John's Jesus, who always seems above it all, admits that his soul is deeply troubled. "And what should I say—'Father, save me from this hour'?" This is as close as John will come to the agony of Jesus at Gethsemane, so acutely portrayed by the other gospels. John, ever determined to emphasize the theological dimension of every moment, allows such a prayer to be only hypothetical on the lips of Jesus. And Jesus follows it immediately and vehemently, "No, it is for this reason that I have come to this hour. Father, glorify your name." In the Gospel of John, the *crucifixion* finds meaning within the context of the *incarnation*. It is the last and most revelatory moment of the incarnation, to be sure. But the word made flesh has always been moving toward "this hour." The life of Jesus, with all its signs and conversations, frames the death of Jesus, even as his death places the final meaning on his life.

"Father, glorify your name," defines what the glorification of the Son of Man really means. Everything Jesus has done is a sign identifying him as the Messiah, the Son of Man. Now in his death, Jesus himself becomes the sign, pointing to the ultimate meaning of all he has done: *the wholly-other glory of the Father*. As *intimate* as he has been with his closest disciples, as *immanent* as he has described his saving presence in human experience (as light, water, bread, etc.), it all points to the final reality of the Father, with whom Christ was in the beginning, before all things were created (1:1). The gospel's ultimate horizon of meaning, the final identity of Christ, and the destiny of all who abide in him—these lie *beyond* our frame of reference.

This is the crowning paradox of our passage. Jesus suddenly turns from his human conversation to conversation with the Father, a prayer penetrating in its urgency. His anxiety in the face of death is transmuted into prayer that God's holy name be glorified. Jesus casts himself upon the Father's will and power to make good on all that has led up to this hour. An escape from death would only render ambiguous and null everything Jesus has done with his life. And everything that Jesus has done with his life points to his life in the Father. This turn in the conversation has the seismic impact of an epiphany. The voice from heaven answers, "I have glorified it, and I will glorify it again." For once, *someone* responds to Jesus at his level of meaning! The voice confirms that the Father has been working through the Son, as Jesus had claimed repeatedly. Moreover, the Father will glorify his name again by raising the Son from the dead. Those standing nearby hear something, but mistake it as thunder, or perhaps the voice of an angel (like so many misunderstandings we have already noted).

With the confirmation of heaven, Jesus now turns back to earth, to enunciate the decisive separation about to take place. Up to this point in the gospel, everything has remained ambiguous to human eyes and misunderstood by human ears. But the impending death of Jesus will remove such ambiguity. "Now is the judgment of this world, now the ruler of this world will be driven out." This is the beginning of the end to Satan's rule of havoc. The light of God's glory in Christ will penetrate the darkness decisively, driving Satan from power. Once this ambiguity has been banished from human eyes, people will see their way to the Son. "And I, when I am lifted up from the earth, will draw all people to myself." One first thinks of the resurrection, but John clarifies (verse 33) that Jesus speaks of the manner of his death, raised up on a cross for all to see.

Jesus abides at the center of a paradox so vast—and so painful—it will stretch him beyond all limits, lift him up from the earth. In the *singularity* of his terrible, lonely death, he will draw *all people* to himself. And each of us, in coming to Christ, will be uniquely caught in the same unbearable paradox, stretched beyond our limits, lifted up with Christ by our own witness to others. Again, "Whoever serves me must follow me, and where I am, there will my servant be also" (12:26).

> **12:34–36:** The crowd answered him, "We have heard from the law that the Messiah remains forever. How can you say that the Son of Man must be lifted up? Who is this Son of Man?" Jesus answered them, "The light is with you for a little longer. Walk while you have the light, so that the darkness may not overtake you. If you walk in the darkness, you do not know where you are going. While you have the light, believe in the light, so that you may become children of light." After Jesus had said this, he departed and hid from them.

The crowd is still lost in ambiguity and confusion, as revealed by their questions. Jesus has apparently left them far behind, as usual. They engage with the statement he made at the beginning of the conversation. The "law" here means Hebrew Scripture generally. It is difficult to find an Old Testament text that would directly support the crowd's impression that "the Messiah remains forever." But there is a strong tradition that God will sustain the line of David eternally (e.g., Psa. 89:4; Isa. 9:7; Ezek. 37:25). The crowd seems to equate the Messiah with the Son of Man. The second question, however, "Who is this Son of Man?" does not fit with the first. Perhaps the "Greeks" are standing at the edges of this conversation, chiming in: what's this "Son of Man" business about?

But Jesus doesn't engage with their confusion. Instead, he exhorts all to walk in the light of his presence while it is still with them, that they may become children of light. But at that very juncture, he leaves and goes into hiding with his inner circle of disciples. The last hours before his arrest will be devoted to a final, extended conversation with them alone.

Reflections from the Quaker Tradition

The central paradox of the Gospel of John, articulated so powerfully in this conversation, constitutes any transformative conversation with Christ. Each will find that paradox, that formation of the cross, in the peculiar circumstances of his or her life. It is sometimes unbearable in its pain and loss. It is other times unbearable in its ecstasy. In both cases, the cross we share with Jesus takes us beyond ourselves to the Father, whose glory shines with unspeakable beauty beyond the world.

Light and seed were central metaphors in early Quaker spiritual counsel. Light suggests the clarity of insight that Christ gives. Seed intimates the being of Christ with us, the new birth raised in us, when we stand still in the light and surrender to God's presence. Isaac Penington wrote evocatively of life in the seed. In his 1661 tract, *Some Directions to the Panting Soul*, Penington counsels forlorn Seekers to abandon their quest:

> The path of life is for the seed of life.... Therefore ... be no more than God hath made thee. Give over thine own willing; give over thine own running; give over thine own desiring to know or to be any thing, and sink down to the seed which God sows in the heart, and let that grow in thee, and be in thee, and breathe in thee, and act in thee, and thou shalt find by sweet experience that the Lord knows that, and loves and owns that, and will lead it to the inheritance of life, which is his portion. And as thou takest up the cross to thyself, and sufferest that to overspread and become a yoke over thee, thou shalt become renewed and enjoy life, and the everlasting inheritance in that [Penington (1994), p. 205].

Jesus speaks of himself as a seed that must fall to the ground and die in order to bear fruit. He also says that his true servants follow him in that surrender. Hence, Penington writes of sinking down to Christ the seed, surrendering even our spiritual ambitions, letting the seed be and act in us, sharing in the cross of Jesus. We shrink from this as from death itself. But it opens to us an abundant and everlasting life.

Early Friends taught that there is only one elect seed, Christ. But that seed indwells with all people. So they rejected the Puritan claim that only some souls are predestined to be saved. They also rejected, however, the illusion that we have the free will to choose and achieve life. The seed is raised up in us only as we surrender our own will, sink down to the seed, and let it grow and reorder our lives. Because this seed is one in all of us, we can feel our unity in that seed.

Edward Burrough was one of the great early leaders of the movement. He was still a teenager when he was convinced by Fox's preaching in 1652. His success in spreading the Quaker message in London was spectacular. One of the early martyrs, Burrough died in London's Newgate prison in 1663, at age twenty-eight. The loss staggered the movement, particularly around London. In response, George Fox wrote a brief epistle "for the staying and settling of Friends' minds":

> Friends, Be still and wait in your own conditions, and settled in the seed of God that doth not change, that in that ye may feel dear Edward Burrough among you in the Seed, in which and by which he begat you to God, with whom he is: and that in the Seed ye may all see and feel him. . . . And so enjoy him in the life that doth not change, but which is invisible [Fox (1952), p. 437].

In Christ the seed, the living and dead are together in one eternal fellowship.

So the friends of Christ share in his cross and in his eternal life. In 1662, while persecutions were at their worst, Fox exhorted Friends to keep meeting, even though they would be rounded up and thrown in prison,

> For God's ways are the truth; and in his power meet, and in his life live, in which you may feed in the pastures . . . [where] Christ is the leader and shepherd . . . know him and his voice; follow him. . . . For all the sufferings are by and through him that is out of the truth; so they that will live godly shall suffer persecution; but you that suffer . . . for truth's sake, the spirit of glory will rest upon you; and if you be evil spoken of for its sake [see Matt. 5:11], being faithful on your parts, Christ is glorified [Fox (1831), 7:238].

God's glory is an unworldly beauty. It is known from a perspective beyond. Those who glorify God may suffer for it. But suffering is not the aim. The aim is to live in

> that wisdom by which all things were created, with which wisdom thou mayest come to be ordered to the glory of the Creator, and with which wisdom thou mayest order all things . . . to the glory of him that created them, and with that thou mayest come to answer the principle of God in every man, that is just, holy, good, and righteous [Fox (1831), 4:231].

That is, to glorify God is to live according to the divine wisdom that created all things (see John 1:3). It is to re-order one's life and one's possessions according to that wisdom. That re-ordered life is a living testimony to God. It speaks to the seed of God in each person. It testifies to the moral nature of reality, and answers the human thirst for that goodness.

Guided Conversation

The following is an opportunity to discern the cross and God's glory in your life.

As with all the meditations in this book, it is important to take time to be quiet. Find a quiet place to sit for twenty to thirty minutes or more. Sit in a comfortable but upright position. Still your body for a few moments. Feel yourself breathing; perhaps notice the pulse somewhere in your body. As you come to a place of quiet, calm awareness say, "Here I am."

Now consider your life: what activities consume your time and energy most intensely? What interests and concerns most occupy your mind? Take a few moments to think of the major ones. These might include your vocation, a primary relationship, or an avocation.

But now consider, which of these passions takes you beyond yourself? Which one is sometimes disturbing in its call to you, its claim on your life? Which one causes you both suffering and joy? Take a few moments to encounter that one great passion. For some, that heat comes out in dramatic ways. For others, it's a quiet but unquenchable fire. Feel in your body its heat, its intensity.

Ask yourself now, does this passion resonate with the Passion of Jesus? Does it embody and express something of God's love working through you? Does it draw you into service to others? Does it stretch you as you are drawn toward opposite but compelling truths, or demands? Does it lift you up, in both agony and ecstasy? Does it take your life as it gives you life? Perhaps not all these descriptions will ring true for you. But your great passion, your life in the cross, should answer to some of them. Take a few moments to feel this fellowship with Christ in his cross.

Now turn it around. How does your great passion help you understand the Passion of Jesus? What insights does it give you into his life and death? Christ's light shining and burning in you helps illuminate his life, just as his life illuminates yours. How does that connection help you understand his fire, his pain, his joy, his hope, his love?

Now, consider this passion your glory. It may not bring you recognition, success, or popularity. It may look like failure, obscurity, rejection—it looked that way at the end of Jesus' life. Maybe only you will recognize its unworldly glory. But it's important for you to recognize it. It's God's glory shining in you. Don't bother yourself with whatever notice the world takes—or doesn't take. This is God's holiness. Keep in holy. It's the one thing you can take with you, rejoining it with the unspeakable joy and immeasurable glory of God.

Finally, take a moment in thankfulness for God's glory in your life. Thank Jesus for showing you the way of faithful stewardship of your measure of that glory. Pray that you may be kept faithful in it.

The Way, the Truth, the Life
John 13:31–14:26

Jesus now speaks to his disciples alone, shortly before his arrest. In this and the succeeding chapter, we will "listen in" on two parts of that conversation. We will notice a shift in the sense of conversation. In earlier conversations, we heard Jesus interact with particular individuals and groups. But we also heard another level—eternal and universal—in the conversation. Now, Jesus speaks more plainly at that second level, describing his relationship with them as it will be after his death. Whatever the disciple John literally heard Jesus say at the end of his life, we find here a more fully literary construction. It decidedly represents the conversation that developed between the risen Christ and the followers who continued meeting in his Spirit and prophesying in his name. It is important to understand that, to the early Church, such prophesy in the Spirit and name of Jesus was as "authentic" as the words Jesus spoke during his life. Thus, for John, this *literary* construction is no less real than the *literal* words of Jesus the night of his arrest. The aim is to bring the listener/reader to the true conversation with Christ.

13:33–38: "Little children, I am with you only a little longer. You will look for me; and as I said to the Jews so now I say to you, 'Where I am going, you cannot come.' I give you a new commandment, that you love one another. Just as I have loved you, you also should love one another. By this everyone will know that you are my disciples, if you have love for one another."

Simon Peter said to him, "Lord where are you going?" Jesus answered, "Where I am going, you cannot follow me now, but you will follow afterward." Peter said to him, "Lord, why can I not follow you now? I will lay down my life for you." Jesus answered "Will you lay down your life for me? Very truly, I tell you, before the cock crows, you will have denied me three times."

Jesus and his disciples have gathered to eat the Passover Seder together. First, he surprises them by washing their feet. Then he shocks them by announcing that one of them will betray him. Then he mystifies them by sending Judas out into the night. Now he confronts them with the news that he is about to leave them. Anticipating their impending pain and confusion, he addresses them tenderly, as "little children." Indeed, as this last conversation with them unfolds, their responses are as naïve as children's.

It probably had not surprised the disciples earlier when Jesus told the religious authorities he was leaving *them* behind (7:33–34). That parting of ways was already painfully evident. But the disciples are unprepared to hear that they too will be left behind. Peter cannot believe that even *he* will be left behind. He vows that he will lay down his life for Jesus. Jesus flatly responds that, to the contrary, Peter will deny him three times. But this is not a rebuke. It is vital that Peter survive this terrible night. Later that evening, during the arrest, Peter will draw a sword and strike the high priest's slave. This time, Jesus *will* rebuke him: "Put your sword back into its sheath. Am I not to drink the cup that the Father has given me?" (18:10–11). Peter has it all wrong. It is not for him to lay down his life for Jesus through an act of violence. Jesus is laying down his life for all.

The disciples have followed Jesus through many strange turns. But they cannot come along this time. He leaves them with a new commandment, to love one another as he has loved them. They must demonstrate toward one another the love with which the Father sent Jesus into the world (3:16). That will demonstrate their authority as his disciples. It will continue the conversation among themselves and with the world. That simple commandment defines with deceptive simplicity the fundamental conversion of faith they are about to experience. Until now, they have been the adoring followers, hanging on his every word and action, but not understanding much. Now they must transfer their devotion from this flesh-and-blood teacher to one another. Everything they have (not really) heard from Jesus must now "come true" among them. Everything that follows in this conversation follows from the new commandment. A painfully wrenching but supremely revelatory moment starts to unfold.

14:1–7: "Do not let your hearts be troubled. Believe in God, believe also in me. In my Father's house there are many dwelling places. If it were not so, would I have told you that I go to prepare a place for you? And if I go and prepare a place for you, I will come again and will take you to myself, so that where I am, there you may be also. And you know the place where I am going." Thomas said to him, "Lord, we do not know where you are going. How can we know the way?" Jesus said to him, "I am the way, and the truth, and the life. No one comes to the Father except through me. If you know me, you will know my Father also. From now on you do know him and have seen him."

Jesus urges them in this crucial hour to believe. Belief here (as always) is more a matter of trust than ideas. No half-understood teaching will carry them through the next twenty-four hours of bewilderment and desolation. They must trust both Jesus and the Father.

Jesus explains that he must leave them in order to prepare a place for them in God's house, where there are many abiding places. Jesus assures them he will return to take them to that place. There, they will be reunited with him. But in Christ, "there" in God's house is also "here" with us. As Augustine eloquently expresses it, Christ prepares the dwelling place by preparing those who will dwell there. Raymond E. Brown (1970, p. 627) remarks similarly that the dwelling place becomes the *indwelling* place Jesus will describe a little later: "Those who love me will keep my word, and my Father will love them, and we will come to them and make our home with them" (14:23). Hence, the dwelling places in the Father's house are as many and diverse as the people with whom God dwells here and now.

Just as Jesus is the *gate* to the sheep (Conversation 7), just as he is the *ladder* between heaven and earth (Conversation 1), he is the *way* between his heavenly Father and his earthly disciples, the portal between eternity and time. He assures them that they already know the place where he is going. But Thomas nervously interjects: they don't know the place, so how can they know the way there? Jesus responds that *the destination and the way there are the same*. The way, truth, and life are one. To know Jesus is to know the Father. There's no other way to the truth. And conversely, there's no truth other than the way there. Truly, it's a way of life.

14:8–14: Philip said to him, "Lord, show us the Father, and we will be satisfied." Jesus said to him, "Have I been with you all this time, Philip, and you still do not know me? Whoever has seen me has seen the Father.

How can you say, 'Show us the Father'? Do you not believe that I am in the Father and the Father is in me? The words that I say to you I do not speak on my own, but the Father who dwells in me does his works. Believe me that I am in the Father and the Father is in me; but if you do not, then believe me because of the works themselves. Very truly, I tell you, the one who believes in me will also do the works that I do and, in fact, will do greater works than these, because I am going to the Father. I will do whatever you ask in my name, so that the Father may be glorified in the Son. If in my name you ask me for anything, I will do it."

Earlier, Thomas (portrayed later, in John 20:24–29, as prone to doubt) fretted that he knew neither the destination nor the route, neither the end nor the means. Now, Philip (perhaps more the idealist?) adds that they would be satisfied *just to see* the destination, the end, the Father. Jesus chides Philip: after all this time together, he still doesn't know Jesus. The disciples had heard Jesus claim his unity with the Father earlier. But they were distracted by the controversy the claim had stirred (10:38–39). They simply sided with their master against his hostile opponents. Now, the imminent departure of Jesus places that truth in a new frame of reference. Jesus now presses them to believe his unity with the Father. He reminds them that his teaching has not been by his own will or wisdom. It has been the Father's action through him. He adds that, if they stumble at simply believing in his unity with the Father, then they may believe on the basis of what they have heard him say and seen him do.

By appealing to his own teaching and works, Jesus brings "life" into focus, relating it to "way" and "truth." That is, Jesus is the *way* to the Father. He is one with the ultimate *truth*. *Life* is the practical way he has demonstrated that truth to the world. But Jesus is about to give up his life, so he speaks of it in the past tense. He shifts emphasis toward the life his disciples will lead without him. He promises to empower them in doing even greater works. But they must ask in his *name*, act in his *authority*. The Father whom Jesus has revealed is thus glorified. Acting in the power of his name, their faith in his unity with the Father will grow to maturity. (Indeed, unless they continue to do the works of Jesus, their belief in him will be empty. That is why Jesus counters the passive mysticism of Philip, who would be satisfied with a vision of the Father.)

In all of this, Jesus establishes the terms of a *new conversation* of faith, to begin after his death. So far, he seems to be disengaging from the disciples: the Son is returning to the Father. In what follows, however, Jesus describes a new intimacy with them.

> **14:15–24:** "If you love me, you will keep my commandments. And I will ask the Father, and he will give you another Advocate, to be with you forever. This is the Spirit of truth, whom the world cannot receive, because it neither sees him nor knows him. You know him, because he abides with you, and he will be in you. I will not leave you orphaned; I am coming to you. In a little while the world will no longer see me, but you will see me; because I live, you also will live. On that day you will know that I am in my Father, and you in me, and I in you. They who have my commandments and keep them are those who love me; and those who love me will be loved by my Father, and I will love them and reveal myself to them." Judas (not Iscariot) said to him, "Lord how is it that you will reveal yourself to us, and not to the world?" Jesus answered him, "Those who love me will keep my word, and my Father will love them and we will come to them. Whoever does not love me does not keep my words; and the word that you hear is not mine, but is from the Father who sent me. I have said these things to you while I am still with you. But the Advocate, the Holy Spirit, whom the Father will send in my name, will teach you everything, and remind you of all that I have said to you."

Jesus continues pressing the matter of works. This time he speaks in terms of keeping his commandments, which will manifest their loving devotion to him. On the basis of their active, practical faith, Jesus will ask the Father to send them the Spirit of truth. In this conversation, the terms shift continually. Works become love. One moment, truth is identified with the transcendent Father. Then truth comes with the Spirit. One moment this Spirit will be their new Advocate, replacing Jesus. The next moment, Jesus promises to be with them himself. Father, Son, Spirit, disciples—all abide in each other. Those who love Jesus will keep his commandments; those who keep his commandments love Jesus. This conversation frustrates anyone looking for a tidy, succinct statement. But this conversation's purpose is to *seal the covenant* with the disciples through a complex *interlacing of all its terms and participants*.

With all this consolidation, however, one great breach takes place. The disciples will be in heightened conflict with the world. Because the world will not receive the Spirit, neither will it see Christ. Judas (not Iscariot) asks how this can be. Jesus explains that the world cannot receive the Spirit because it neither loves Christ nor keeps his commandments. Again, *practical works of love* are the basis for a living faith. The Hebrew verb for "covenant-making" (*berith*) means both "to cut" and "to bind." The very action that binds the disciples closer to Jesus and one another will also divide them more strongly from the world at large.

"Peace I leave with you, my peace I give to you. I do not give to you as the world gives. Do not let your hearts be troubled, and do not let them be afraid" (John 14:28). Jesus contrasts his peace with the way the world offers peace. He speaks these words in an obscure province of the mighty Roman Empire. In that day, many praised Rome for bringing peace and stability to an ancient world chronically at war. Yet Rome established peace through military conquest and ruthless, violent repression. Indeed, within the next few hours, Jesus would become one more victim of *Pax Romana*, which had already crucified thousands of his fellow Jews. Crucifixion was a horrific form of public execution, employed to dampen rebellion. When Jesus spoke of the way the world gives peace, *Pax Romana* was the prime example. He offered his disciples a peace opposite to the peace that power enforces. Ironically, *Pax Christi* broke out *precisely* through the death of Jesus at Roman hands. And *Pax Christi* spread through the disciples' proclamation of his death, *blatantly* in the face of Roman power, condemning "the ruler of this world" before the eyes of growing thousands.

Reflections from the Quaker Tradition

William Dewsbury was one of the early Quaker prophets of the 1650s. In the 1640s, however, he had been a soldier in the English Civil War. He had fought in Parliament's army for the cause of religious freedom and political reform. Like many young, idealistic Puritans, he was certain of God's favor for Parliament and the justness of the war. But early in the war's progress, he heard the word of the Lord:

> Put up thy Sword into thy Scabard, if my Kingdom were of this World, then would my Children Fight . . . which Word enlightened my Heart,

and discovered the mystery of iniquity, and that the Kingdom of Christ was within; and the Enemies was within, and was spiritual, and my Weapons against them must be spiritual, the Power of God [quoted in Gwyn (2000), p. 224–25].

Dewsbury heard the Advocate speak to him the same words Jesus spoke to Peter (noted above), and later to Pilate (see Conversation 11). He didn't abandon the struggle for reform. But he now understood the nature of true, redemptive conflict. Christ forbade him to fight any longer against flesh and blood. He returned home to Yorkshire to await further guidance. By 1652, he was part of an emerging Quaker vanguard. Early Friends called their struggle the "Lamb's War" (for a treatment of early Quaker spiritual politics, see Gwyn, 1995). It was a nonviolent answer to the hollow victory of the Civil War, which failed to produce reform. The Lamb's War attracted a number of ex-soldiers disillusioned with Parliament's failure to grant promised freedoms. These men had learned that true social transformation must be wrought from the inside out, and from the grassroots up, through intense spiritual struggle. They fought by speaking truth to power. The government violently repressed the Quaker movement. Hostile mobs also attacked Quaker preachers and meetings. But the tactics of the Lamb's War remained nonviolent. The Quaker commitment to Christian pacifism was an officially published testimony by 1661. Quaker peace witness today generates creative alternatives to violence at every level of society (see Conversation 11).

Edward Hicks is one of our Quaker enigmas. He was a beloved minister among Friends in Bucks County, Pennsylvania in the early nineteenth century. When he died in 1849, hundreds attended his memorial meeting, remembering him as a preacher. But today he is known for his primitive art, particularly for his sixty-one renditions of Isaiah's prophecy (Isa. 11:1–9). He titled these paintings "The Peaceable Kingdom." (See an example below.) Hicks had been apprenticed as a boy to a decorative painter. In adulthood he supported himself and his family (not very successfully) as a farmer and sign-painter. But Hicks' artwork was studiously ignored by Friends. Early Quakers, arising from the poor, rural North, had associated art with the arrogant, conspicuous consumption of the rich, just as they associated music and dance with the desperate frolic of tavern life. The Religious Society of Friends continued to spurn music and art until the latter nineteenth century, when first evangelical and then liberal reformers relaxed the discipline.

Isaiah's eschatological fable of animals at peace with one another was the guiding vision of Hicks' life. The reconciliation of opposites—the wolf and the lamb, the leopard and the kid, the lion and the ox, the cow and the bear—provided him solace during an era of controversy and schism in American Quakerism. His cousin, Elias Hicks, another minister and Long Island farmer, was at the center of the controversies. Edward had a volatile temper and was repeatedly drawn into heated defenses of his cousin. These occasions only deepened his grief at the Quaker schism, which finally took place in 1827.

Hicks' paintings typically include as background a scene of William Penn signing his treaty with the Delaware Indians in 1682. It offers a reminder that the Peaceable Kingdom actually does break forth in this world. During his remaining twenty-two years after the Hicksite Separation, Edward slowly gained the inner peace he had idealized in oils so many times. In a recorded sermon, given at the Goose Creek

Meeting in Virginia in 1837, Hicks laid out his understanding of Isaiah's vision. He understood the animals to symbolize different human personality types. He viewed the predatory animals as embodiments of the four humors in classical and medieval thought. The wolf is melancholy, the leopard sanguine, the bear phlegmatic, and the lion choleric. The goal of each is to be reconciled with its opposite, to be restored to personal health and communal peace.

In particular, Hicks understood his own personality as tending to the lion's violent anger. He longed to be reconciled to the personality of the ox. In this sermon, he refers particularly to a certain Quaker elder who had been a mentor to him: "a man of choleric complexion, and in his first nature like a lion; but when I knew him he was as patient, submissive, and powerful as an ox. He was truly a precious father, taking me by the hand in my youth, and leading by precept and example" [quoted in Mather (1970), p. 32]. Edward Hicks' witness is a good illustration of Raymond Brown's comment (noted above) that Christ prepares a place for us by preparing a place within us. As we live toward the best and sweetest of God's promises, impossible and otherworldly as they seem, something of that beauty grows within us.

Guided Conversation

There is a saying among peace activists: "There is no way to peace; peace is the way." That turn-of-phrase captures something of the truth Jesus witnesses in this conversation. The following is an opportunity to taste that reality in Christ.

As with all the meditations in this book, it is important to take time to be quiet. Find a quiet place to sit for twenty to thirty minutes or more. Sit in a comfortable but upright position. Still your body for a few moments. Feel yourself breathing; perhaps notice the pulse somewhere in your body. As you come to a place of quiet, calm awareness say, "Here I am."

Now consider a matter in your life that disturbs your peace of mind. Maybe something in the future you dread. Maybe a present crisis making you anxious. Maybe something in the past you cannot lay to rest. Focus on one such thing and contemplate it for a few moments. Don't entangle yourself in it. Keep a little distance from it and see it clearly.

What is the quality of that matter? What word or phrase captures what troubles you about it? What about this matter blocks your way to peace? When you have found the word or phrase that fits, stay with it a few moments, to see if it continues to feel right. If it doesn't, wait to find one that does.

Now ask, why is it that way? What makes it so uncomfortable? so insurmountable? so defeating? Wait for an answer. The answer is not an explanation. It is more a sense of the matter's true nature.

You may feel something in you shift as you sit with that question. A sense of peace may come over you. That sense of peace comes from beyond—or below—your understanding. Remember that Christ's way of being with us and teaching us is incarnational. It usually abides below the level of rational thought. Wait for it.

Peace is here with you now. As you become aware of peace, it may reveal a way to deal with your dilemma. It may lead you to offer someone comfort, forgiveness, reconciliation, a fresh start. It may lead you into some plain speaking, even confrontation. But it will not lead you to do emotional or physical violence.

If you find the peace of Christ abiding with you in this meditation, stay quietly with it as long as you are able. You might offer thanks for whatever comfort or guidance you have received, ask Christ to accompany you, or ask Christ to continue leading you to the Father.

CONVERSATION 10

Friends

John 15:1–17

Jesus now ceases referring to the Spirit as another Advocate to replace him after he is gone. He speaks of his own direct relationship with them, with an intimacy he has not previously broached with them. He speaks now as if he is already gone in the flesh and present with them in the Spirit. This passage in John is more obviously the product of later Christian prophecy in the Spirit and name of Jesus. There are no more questions or comments from the disciples. He now speaks fully through them, rather than to them. In other words, this passage is the product of an ongoing conversation among the disciples of Jesus, as he abides in them and speaks through them.

That shift is signaled by the words of Jesus at the end of Chapter 14: "Rise, let us be on our way" (14:31). Because the conversation continues without mention of a change of location, many commentators have assumed that a sloppy editor neglected to edit out what must have been an earlier end to the conversation, before they went to the garden (see 18:1). But, as William Countryman suggests (1994: pp. 105–06), Jesus beckons his disciples (and us) to rise to another level of understanding. As we noted near the beginning of Conversation 1, that *anagogical* (literally, "leading up") moment is where we rise to mystical or apocalyptic insight, where the conversation between Jesus and the disciples becomes our conversation with Christ.

> **15:1–6:** "I am the true vine, and my Father is the vinegrower. He removes every branch in me that bears no fruit. Every branch that bears fruit he prunes [literally, cleanses] to make it bear more fruit. You have already been cleansed by the word that I have spoken to you. Abide in me as I abide in you. Just as the branch cannot bear fruit by itself unless it abides in the vine, neither can you unless you abide in me. I am the vine, you are the branches. Those who abide in me and I in them bear much

fruit, because apart from me you can do nothing. Whoever does not abide in me is thrown away like a branch and withers; such branches are gathered, thrown into the fire, and burned."

With another "I am" statement, Jesus returns to the earthly metaphors that characterized earlier conversations. The image of the vine and branches is one of the richest in John's gospel, suggesting intimacy, nurture, fecundity. Abiding in Christ the vine is the basis of a fruitful life. It is true life.

The image of the Father as vine-dresser introduces a theme of judgment. The dynamics of judgment here are the same we saw in Conversation 2. That is, just as those who do the truth come further into the light, fruitful branches abide in the vine and will be pruned for greater fruitfulness. Conversely, just as those whose deeds are evil run from the light, so branches become unfruitful because they have already lost connection with the vine. So they are cut off, gathered up, and burned. Is this a warning of "hell-fire," or simply an extension of the vinicultural metaphor?

The pruning/cleansing of branches to produce greater fruitfulness suggests that even fruitful Christian life has its rigors. At times, growth in Christ involves hardships and losses that may appear disturbingly like judgment. Such experiences of personal darkness and stripping, if endured in hope, lead to deeper, more fruitful faith. Jesus assures his disciples that they have already been cleansed by the word he has spoken to them.

> **15:7-11:** "If you abide in me, and my words abide in you, ask for whatever you wish, and it will be done for you. My Father is glorified by this, that you bear much fruit and become my disciples. As the Father has loved me, so I have loved you; abide in my love. If you keep my commandments, you will abide in my love, just as I have kept my Father's commandments and abide in his love. I have said these things to you so that my joy may be in you, and that your joy may be complete."

Jesus expands upon what it means to abide in the vine. First, living in his presence empowers fruitfulness: one need only ask for his help. Second, this fruitful abiding *glorifies* the Father, in whose authority Jesus has called and teaches his disciples. Third, as Jesus kept his Father's *commandments* and remained in his *love*, so the disciples will abide in his love as they keep his commandments. And fourth, the *joy* of the Son in the Father will be fulfilled in the disciples through these things.

> **15:12–17:** "This is my commandment, that you love one another as I have loved you. No one has greater love than this, to lay down one's life for one's friends. You are my friends if you do what I command you. I do not call you servants any longer, because the servant does not know what the master is doing; but I have called you friends, because I have made known to you everything that I have heard from my Father. You did not choose me but I chose you. And I appointed you to go and bear fruit, fruit that will last, so that the Father will give you whatever you ask him in my name. I am giving you these commands so that you may love one another."

With the theme of joy, the conversation moves to a deeper level. Jesus commands his disciples to love one another with the same love they have already received from him. He is about to demonstrate to them the full extent of his love by laying down his life for them, his "friends" (or "beloved"—the Greek is *philoi*). There is a tension here between *unconditional* and *conditional* love. He has *already* chosen them and loved them; he is laying down his life for them. Still, they will fulfill his love and manifest themselves as his friends *if* they follow his commands. The intimacy of friendship with Christ takes them beyond servanthood, apprenticeship. He imparts to his friends the full revelation he has known with the Father. But he emphasizes that this has been his initiative. He has *chosen* them as his friends and *appointed* them to bear fruit that abides. So their *being* and their *doing* are grounded in Christ. Consequently, through their friendship with Christ, and in their striving to be fruitful in Christ, the Father will give them whatever they ask. Finally, as they experience themselves as branches of the same vine, they are empowered to enact Christ's love among themselves.

Scholars have noted a literary structure in 15:7–17 called *chiasm*. A chiastic pattern is one in which a sequence of elements is repeated (sometimes in negative terms) in reverse order. This pattern is common in biblical and classical literature. I have slightly adapted below Raymond Brown's diagram of the structure (Brown, 1970, p. 667):

verse 7–10	verses 12–17
7: If... my words abide in you	**17:** I give you these commandments...
7: ask... it will be done for you	**16:** the Father will give you whatever...
8: bear fruit	**16:** bear fruit
8: become my disciples	**16:** I chose you
9: the Father has loved me	**15:** I reveal everything... from the Father
9: I have loved you	**15:** I have called you my friends
10: remain in my love—keep my commandments	**12:** you are my friends if you do what I command you

verse 11: I have said these things to you so that my joy may be in you

Joy functions as the "hinge" of the chiastic sequence. The practical aspect of keeping the love commandment of Christ (whereby Christ's word abides in the disciples) forms the beginning and end of the sequence.

Texts like the Gospel of John were typically heard, rather than read, by early Christians. Many were illiterate, and copies of the gospels were rare in any case. Chiastic structures like this one are found frequently in biblical and classical texts, partly because they helped hearers to memorize stories or teachings. So chiastic structuring of texts had a practical, mnemonic purpose. But chiasm also has a deeper significance. It often seems intended to highlight the hidden nature of a matter, or the most decisive element in a story or an exposition.

For example, the Book of Revelation is structured chiastically. It begins and ends with messages from John (probably someone other than the writer of the Fourth Gospel) to Christian communities struggling under persecution. But following his introductory call to resistance, the prophet offers a series of cosmic, symbolic visions, culminating in a portrayal of the fundamental conflict between God and the dragon (Chapters 12–14). The bizarre and exalted imageries of that "hinge" section unveil (the literal meaning of "apocalypse") the true nature of the Christian community's struggle with Rome. The ensuing sections portray God's victory over the dragon, the two beasts, and Babylon, until John finally engages the churches again at "ground-level" in the book's conclusion.

In this conversation, Jesus similarly begins by stressing practical, this-worldly service within the Christian community, empowered by prayer. He then speaks of the love he has passed on to them. The joy of love and service forms the heart of the message. After revealing that innermost meaning, Jesus declares that they have become his friends. Their prayers in his name will empower them to love/serve one another in practical ways.

This discourse on the vine forms the centerpiece of the parting words to the disciples (John 13–17). And at the heart of this discourse, Jesus describes the joy of his continuing relationship with them. There is artful literary construction here on John's part. But the *literary* structure serves to highlight the *spiritual truth* of abiding in Christ. In other words, the *sequence of words* intimates the *presence of the living word* in and among Christ's friends. Even if the reader/hearer knows nothing about chiasm, the structure of this great passage communicates its effects upon human consciousness.

The remainder of John 15 places Christ's love within the community in sharp contrast to the *hatred* they will experience from the world. The world will persecute them because it hated and persecuted Jesus first. In John, the beloved community and the rest of the world seem to exist in nearly dualistic opposition to each other. (We saw a near-dualism in Conversation 2 with Nicodemus. But we found the dualism grounded in human movement either from or toward the light.) The dualistic sense is heightened by assertions that Jesus has loved and chosen these friends. Still, we recall that God's love for the whole world has sent the Son into the world (3:16). So election stands in tension with universal love in John.

Reflections from the Quaker Tradition

Among the generation of Seekers who formed the early Quaker movement, some powerful friendships were forged. Edward Burrough and Francis Howgill, natives of Westmorland in the North, became yoke-fellows in ministry. In the summer of 1654, they initiated the Quaker mission in London, which was an immediate sensation. The work of preaching, counseling, debating, and publishing was intense and relentless. Although Howgill was sixteen years Burrough's senior, the two formed a deep bond. They shared long hours of work and waged many spiritual struggles with Puritan divines bent on discrediting and persecuting them. As noted in Conversation 8, Burrough died in London's Newgate prison in 1663. Howgill wrote of Burrough, comparing their friendship in spiritual "battle" to that of David and Jonathan. When Jonathan was slain at Mount Gilboa, David lamented, "The beauty of Israel is slain upon high places." Francis testified, "Precious in the Eyes of the Lord and surely precious wast thou to me, O dear Edward, I am distressed for thee my brother, very pleasant hast thou been to me, and my love to thee was wonderful, passing the love of Women, oh thou whose Bow never turned back" [see 2 Sam. 1:17–27]. These words appear in the opening pages of Burrough's collected works, published in 1672. By that time, Howgill too had perished in prison.

We have already heard some of Isaac and Mary Penington's witness. Both had spent long, troubled years seeking in London, before they were reached by the Quaker movement. They married in 1654. Mary remembers that she found in Isaac a soulmate in the search for truth:

> My love was drawn to him because I found he saw the deceit in all notions, and lay as one who refused to be comforted by any appearance of religion, until he came to his temple, "who is truth and no lie." All things that appeared to be religion and were not so, were manifest to him; so that, till then, he was sick and weary of all appearances. My heart was united to him, and a desire was in me to be serviceable to him in his desolate condition, for he was alone and miserable in this world, and I gave up much to be a companion to him in his suffering [Mary Penington (1992), pp. 38–39].

In the Quaker movement they eventually found the authentic faith they craved. Imprisonments damaged Isaac's health over the years. He died at home in 1679, at age sixty-three. Mary wrote:

> Ah me! he is gone! He that none exceeded in kindness, in tenderness, in love inexpressible to the relation as a wife. Next to the love of God in Christ Jesus to my soul, was his love precious and delightful to me. My bosom-one! that was as my guide and counsellor! My pleasant companion! My tender sympathizing friend! As near to the sense of my pain, sorrow, grief, and trouble as it was possible. Yet this great help and benefit is gone . . . such was the great kindness the Lord shewed me in that hour, that my spirit ascended with him in that very moment

that his spirit left his body; and I saw him safe in his own mansion, and rejoiced with him, and was at that instant gladder of it, than ever I was of enjoying him in the body. . . . This testimony to dear Isaac Penington is from the greatest loser of all that had a share in his life, Mary Penington [Isaac Penington (1995), pp. 444–45].

Such friendship grows as we are united at a level deeper than our own thoughts, feelings, and motivations—as we are joined together in the vine.

That union is grounded in the experience of worship. Perhaps no writer has described the experience of Quaker worship better than Thomas Kelly (1893–1941). The last few years of his short life were particularly radiant with the joy Jesus describes to his friends in this conversation. In his essay, "The Gathered Meeting," Kelly begins,

In the practice of group worship on the basis of silence come special times when the electric hush and solemnity and depth of power steals over the worshipers. A blanket of divine covering comes over the room, a stillness that can be felt is over all, and the worshipers are gathered into a unity and synthesis of life which is amazing indeed. A quickening Presence pervades us, breaking down some part of the special privacy and isolation of our individual lives and blending our spirits within a superindividual Life and Power. An objective, dynamic Presence enfolds all, nourishes our souls, speaks glad, unutterable comfort within us, and quickens us in depths that had before been slumbering. The Burning Bush has been kindled in our midst, and we stand together on holy ground [Kelly (1977), p. 86].

Such meetings for worship may or may not include vocal ministry spoken out of the silence:

Certainly the deepness of the covering of a meeting is not proportional to the number of words spoken. A gathered meeting may proceed entirely in silence, rolling on with increasing depth and intensity until the meeting breaks and tears are furtively brushed away. Such really powerful hours of unbroken silence frequently carry a genuine progression of spiritual change and experience. . . . Outwardly, all silences seem alike, as all minutes are alike by the clock. But inwardly the Divine Leader of worship directs us through progressive unfoldings of ministration, and may in silence bring an inward climax which is as definite as the climax of the Mass, when the host is elevated in adoration. But more frequently some words are spoken.... I have particularly in mind those hours of worship in which no one person, no one speech, stands out as the one that "made" the meeting, those hours wherein the personalities that take part verbally are not enhanced as individuals in the eyes of others, but are subdued and softened, and lost sight of because, in the language of Fox, "The Lord's Power was over all." [pp. 99–100]

Of course, not every meeting for worship attains such depth. Kelly emphasizes that the outcome of worship is less important than the intention we bring to it.

But what if the meeting has not been a gathered meeting? Are those meetings failures that have not been hushed by a covering? Quite definitely they are not. If we have been faithful, we may go home content and nourished from any meeting. . . . The crux of religious living lies in the will, not in transient and variable states. Utter dedication to the will of God is open to all, for every man can will, and can will his will into the will of God. . . . Some hours of worship are full of glow and life, but others lack the quality. The disciplined soul, and the disciplined group, have learned to cling to the reality of God's presence, whether the feeling of presence is great or faint. If only the group has been knit about the very springs of motivation, the fountain of the will, then real worship has taken place [pp. 102–104].

The uniting of wills in the discipline of worship engenders true friendship in the eternal. And from the timeless, our timely care for one another grows organically. We become fruitful branches of the vine. As Isaac Penington reminded Friends in Amersham in a 1667 letter, "Our life is love, and peace, and tenderness; and bearing one with another, and forgiving one another, and not laying accusations one against the other; but praying for one another, and helping one another up with a tender hand" [quoted in Britain Yearly Meeting (1995), 10:1].

Friendship in the eternal is not, of course, limited to relationships within a given faith community. Just as the true shepherd has sheep "not of this fold," friendship forges bonds in a vine whose true extent we never fully know. Friendship is subversive of the social boundaries and hierarchies that typically separate us. Over the centuries, Friends have formed deep friendships and collaborated with others in work for peace, racial justice, women's rights, prison reform, gay rights, sustainable living, and many other areas of social concern. Answering that of God in all kinds of people, we find allies and soulmates in a larger pattern the world cannot contain.

Guided Conversation

What follows is a *chiastic* meditation. The sequence of steps is aimed to offer a personal experience that parallels the literary structure we observed in this conversation. Although the elements here do not exactly follow those of the passage, this meditation similarly turns on the experience of joy. While the term, chiasm, may be new for the reader, the experience of this meditation may feel familiar.

As with all the meditations in this book, it is important to take time to be quiet. Find a quiet place to sit for twenty to thirty minutes or more. Sit in a comfortable but upright position. Still your body for a few moments. Feel yourself breathing; perhaps notice the pulse somewhere in your body. As you come to a place of quiet, calm awareness say, "Here I am."

As you become still and centered, find a sense of Christ there at the center of your being. Abide with Christ there for a few moments.

Now, bring to mind a friend, someone dear to you. It might be a member of your faith community, but doesn't need to be. Take a few moments to savor that person and your friendship with him or her. Simply appreciate it. As you abide in Christ, enjoy your connection with that person.

Now take a few moments to consider: does this friendship make you more whole? Does it make you a more fruitful branch of the vine? As you abide in that love, you could give thanks for your friend, and for your friendship.

Now, what is your heart's desire for your friend? What is your friend's particular need or hope at this time? If you feel that desire on his or her behalf, ask God to fulfill it. Ask simply and whole-heartedly. When you feel you have asked truly, just sit a moment with that.

Feel the joy of Christ in you. Feel the joy of your love for your friend. Feel the joy of your prayer for him or her. Stay with that joy for a few moments.

Now consider that Christ has laid down his life for your friend, and for you. Consider that Jesus died to point you toward God's truth, and to free you from delusion and sin. Consider how Christ lays down his life for you by patiently abiding in you, no matter how distracted and inconsiderate you may be at times. Take a moment to consider this wondrous gift.

Now consider whether Christ may be leading you to lay down your life for your friend. What patience on your part is needed at this time? What act of kindness or practical help might you offer? Take a few moments to await an answer. It may be clear and specific, or just a general sense.

As that sense emerges, ask Christ to help you fulfill that act of friendship. Ask for the courage, generosity, truthfulness, patience, or whatever you need in following that leading. What might be the first step?

Remember, of course, that friendship is consensual. What you feel led to offer may not be accepted, at least at this time. If you offer something that your friend rejects, consider it possible that you have mistaken your leading. Return to Christ again in prayer. Or seek the counsel of another trusted friend or mentor.

Pilate

John 18:28–19:16

W e come now to the last major conversation before Jesus' death. The trial before Pilate is much extended in John, compared with the first three gospels. John also seems to presuppose our previous knowledge of the trial, because he never explains who Pilate is, or gives us the fuller name, "Pontius Pilate." It appears that one aim of this highly structured conversation is to dramatize the relation between Christ and worldly political authority, with implications for the way followers should respond when faced with the threat of persecution.

At first glance, Pilate seems to be sympathetic to Jesus. He appears to be badgered by the chief priests into executing him, despite his better judgment. But we have seen much irony in the conversations in John. Nowhere is that irony richer (or more painful) than in Pilate's conversation with Jesus. Like those who appear earlier in John, Pilate will misunderstand Jesus' words, and will say things truer than he himself intends. But we shall also find Pilate to be a shrewd manipulator who utilizes Jesus as a pawn in a larger political game with local authorities.

John makes Rome fully complicit in the death of Jesus. Only in his story is Jesus arrested by a combined force of Roman soldiers and Jewish police. In John, the priests only question Jesus. They do not try him. And in John, it is the Romans who beat and abuse Jesus. John's case against the chief priests and Pharisees runs throughout his entire gospel. But when the Romans finally enter the drama, John portrays them no less scathingly.

18:28–32: Then they took Jesus from Caiaphas to Pilate's headquarters. It was early in the morning. They themselves did not enter the headquarters, so as to avoid ritual defilement and to be able to eat the Passover. So Pilate went out to them and said, "What accusation do you bring against this man?" They answered," If this man were not a criminal, we would not have handed him over to you." Pilate said to them, "Take him yourselves and judge him according to your law." The Jews replied, "We are not permitted to put anyone to death." (This was to fulfill what Jesus had said when he indicated the kind of death he was to die.)

We will see a strange movement back and forth, in and out of the Roman headquarters (the *Praetorium*) throughout this story. First, Pilate must come out to meet with the Jewish leaders, who have brought Jesus with urgency, early in the morning, hoping to dispatch him before the Passover proceeds any further. Their words are full of innuendo. They suggest that he is a criminal so dangerous that Pilate should execute him right away. They do not describe his crime but imply political overtones. Pilate teases them with a needless question. He fully knows they lack the authority to execute criminals. He simply wants to make them say it, to admit their impotence, their subordination to Rome.

18:33–40: Then Pilate entered the headquarters again, summoned Jesus, and asked him, "Are you the King of the Jews?" Jesus answered, "Do you ask this on your own, or did others tell you about me?" Pilate replied, "I am not a Jew, am I? Your own nation and chief priests have handed you over to me. What have you done?" Jesus answered, "My kingdom is not from this world. If my kingdom were from this world, my followers would be fighting to keep me from being handed over to the Jews. But as it is, my kingdom is not from here." Pilate asked him, "So you are a king?" Jesus answered, "You say that I am a king. For this I was born and for this I came into the world, to testify to the truth. Everyone who belongs to the truth listens to my voice." Pilate asked him, "What is truth?" After this, he went out to the Jews again and told them, "I find no case against him. But you have a custom that I release someone for you at the Passover. Do you want me to release for you the King of the Jews?" They shouted in reply, "Not this man, but Barabbas!" Now Barabbas was a bandit.

Inside his headquarters, Pilate questions Jesus for himself. He evidently has heard reports that Jesus claims to be King of the Jews. That is the only question about Jesus that concerns him. Jesus asks where Pilate heard that accusation. Pilate snaps back contemptuously that he is no Jew. He couldn't care less about Jewish affairs, except as they impinge upon Roman power and authority. But it's remarkable that the priestly collaborationist regime has handed Jesus over to him. So what has he done?

Jesus responds by answering Pilate's first question, regarding his kingship. His kingdom is not of the same order as Rome's. If he were competing with Rome, his followers would have fought to resist his arrest. (John may well intend these words as a renunciation of violence by Christians generally, and not regarding the arrest of Jesus only.) Like so many of Jesus' interlocutors, Pilate gropes for his meaning: so you *are* a king. Jesus wryly remarks that Pilate has said so (even if he doesn't understand). He then goes on to answer Pilate's second question ("What have you done?"). The nature of his kingly authority is totally divorced from coercive power. Jesus simply testifies to the truth (a truth not from this world). Those who belong to the truth, who know its authority, heed his voice. (This statement parallels his remark to Nicodemus, regarding human responses to the light.) Pilate famously spits, "What is truth?" In so saying, he demonstrates that he does not belong to that realm. He scorns truth's authority. He knows, obeys, and exercises power—violent, coercive power. Power from this world.

Pilate goes back out to talk with the local leaders. They scrupulously maintain their cultic purity by remaining outside his precinct, even as they seek his help in executing Jesus. Pilate baits them, claiming that he finds no case against Jesus. Going further, he wants to see just how badly they want Jesus dead. He could release their "King" in honor of their Passover. Incensed, they shout back that they would rather he free Barabbas, a bandit. The Greek *lestes* could denote a common criminal or a Zealot guerrilla fighter. Pilate knows the priests loathe both bandits and freedom fighters as much as he does. It's clear now just how desperately they want to be rid of Jesus.

> **19:1–6:** Then Pilate took Jesus and had him flogged. And the soldiers wove a crown of thorns and put it on his head, and they dressed him in a purple robe. They kept coming up to him, saying, "Hail, King of the Jews!" and striking him on the face. Pilate went out again and said to them, "Look I am bringing him out to you to let you know that I find no case against him." So Jesus came out, wearing the crown of thorns and the purple robe. Pilate said to them, "Here is the man!" When the chief priests and the police saw him, they shouted, "Crucify him! Crucify him!" Pilate said to them, "Take him yourselves and crucify him. I find no case against him."

The flogging is often interpreted as Pilate's effort to spare Jesus' life, to appease the priests' wrath. But it would be against Roman law to scourge an innocent man. David Rensberger (*The Johannine Faith and Liberating Community* [Westminster, 1988], pp. 93–94) argues convincingly that Pilate's real intention is to humiliate the Jewish leaders. The crown of thorns, the purple robe, the mocking salutations and physical abuse by the soldiers all combine to make a cruel travesty of Jewish kingship and nationalism. Jesus himself is barely a consideration to Pilate. He is simply a handy "whipping boy," useful to mock these subordinate local rulers. So Pilate trots Jesus out as a hapless mock-king: "Here is the man!" Pilate's stigmatization of Jesus renders him even more blasphemous to "the Jews," who shout to have him crucified-effaced. Jesus has become an abomination kicked back and forth between antagonized political powers. Again, Pilate tells the priests to go crucify him themselves. This not only reminds them again of their powerlessness to execute Jesus. It accentuates the situation: they would have Pilate inflict a hideous Roman punishment upon Jesus, one they would never dare enact themselves, even if they could. They want him to do their dirty work.

> **19:7–12:** The Jews answered him, "We have a law, and according to that law he ought to die because he claimed to be the Son of God." Now when Pilate heard this he was more afraid than ever. He entered his headquarters again and asked Jesus, "Where are you from?" But Jesus gave him no answer. Pilate therefore said to him, "Do you refuse to speak to me? Do you not know that I have power to release you, and power to crucify you?" Jesus answered him, "You would have no power over me unless it had been given you from above; therefore the one who handed me over to you is guilty of a greater sin." From then on Pilate tried to release him, but the Jews cried out, "If you release this man, you are no friend of the emperor. Everyone who claims to be a king sets himself against the emperor."

The authorities respond to Pilate's taunt that according to their law, he should die for claiming to be the Son of God. This is an abrupt shift in tactics. Up to this point, they have attributed political aspirations to Jesus. The theological claim, Son of God, genuinely worries Pilate. Rensberger (p. 94) argues that in verse 8, the Greek *mallon* should be translated to suggest that Pilate "became afraid *instead*," rather than "became *more* afraid." This is an abrupt change in mood. His treatment of Jesus and his accusers up to this point has been high-handed and cynical. He toys with this pathetic pretender and his accusers. But Pilate has seen from previous experience how much trouble he stirs when he affronts these people's religious sensibilities. According to the Jewish historian Josephus, massive riots broke out in Jerusalem when Pilate placed Roman standards in the Temple precincts.

So Pilate retreats back inside his headquarters to confront Jesus more seriously. He asks the question that has swirled around Jesus throughout John's gospel, "Where are you from?" He is offended that he receives no answer. He reminds Jesus that he holds over him the power of life or (terrible) death. Jesus responds with typical irony: Pilate has no power but what has been given him from above. Is this "above" heaven, or simply the Roman chain of command to which Pilate is answerable? In either case, Jesus has demeaned him as a mere functionary who has blundered—however cruelly—into affairs he does not understand. "Therefore," Jesus adds, those who have some understanding of God (the theological "above"), and yet have handed him over to Pilate, are the guiltier parties.

The topic of culpability, whether religious or simply bureaucratic, makes Pilate still more uneasy. He re-emerges from his headquarters determined to release Jesus. The Jewish authorities realize that raising a religious issue has proven counterproductive. So they play their political trump-card. Pilate is no friend of Caesar (the political "above") if he releases a reputed King of the Jews. Within the Roman system of political patronage, to be a "friend of Caesar" was a matter of loyalty in exchange for favor. The entire Empire functioned by means of an elaborate structure of such hierarchically defined "friendships." (Note the contrast implied here with the intimate friendship between Jesus and his disciples in the preceding conversation.)

19:13-16: When Pilate heard these words, he brought Jesus outside and sat on the judge's bench at the place called The Stone Pavement, or in Hebrew Gabbatha. Now it was the day of Preparation for the Passover, and it was about noon. He said to the Jews, "Here is your King!" They cried out, "Away with him! Away with him! Crucify him!" Pilate asked them, "Shall I crucify your King?" The chief priests answered, "We have no king but the emperor." Then he handed him over to them to be crucified.

Even in their subordinate position, the priestly collaborationists have found the argument that bends Pilate to their desires. Any report to his superiors of leniency toward Jesus could ruin him. He brings Jesus out, ready to strike a deal. These negotiations, which began early in the morning, have dragged on until noon. The fullest light of day now exposes all parties for who they are. Pilate taunts the Jewish leaders once more, presenting Jesus before them as "your King." They cannot bear the sight of this bloody, degraded figure dressed in purple. They vehemently demand that Pilate do *away* with him. But Pilate continues to provoke them. He wants to extract something from them in return for executing Jesus. Finally, to end this political charade, the chief priests say what Pilate wants to hear: "We have no king but the emperor." Traditionally Jews affirmed the Lord to be their only king. Indeed, that affirmation was part of the liturgy of Passover, just underway. But, to get this business finished, the chief priests submit to this final humiliation through this pledge of allegiance. It's already noon, and they have major responsibilities for these holy days. The quickness with which Pilate hands Jesus over for execution is the final indication that his demurrals have been cynically manipulative. Surely, he too has other business to transact today.

Jesus has barely participated in this conversation. This most political moment in John's gospel amounts almost entirely to brokerage between the "real" powers in Judea. There is nothing left for Jesus to say to the chief priests. The few remarks he makes to Pilate "speak truth to power" in the tersest terms. He exposes Pilate's authority as a wearisome set of negotiations that has consumed an entire morning. Pilate is a mere functionary in a drama he doesn't even understand. In the very act of exercising political acumen and power, even in abusing Jesus for the sake of humiliating these bothersome collaborationists, Pilate himself becomes the pawn. The trial of Jesus (when we read it with the ironic sense we learn to expect from John) is *a revelatory moment, a high-noon deconstruction of the political in light of the truth*. Every confrontation John's community experiences with civil authority will be understood in that penetrating light. They may be stripped, beaten, mocked, even killed like Jesus. But the emperor's friend is truly the one without clothes.

Reflections from the Quaker Tradition

The first two generations of Friends suffered systematic persecution for their controversial faith. From the beginnings of the movement around 1652 until official toleration in 1689, more than 20,000 Friends suffered at least one imprisonment in England and Wales (out of an estimated 60,000 Quakers in Britain at the time). At least 450 died, mostly from septic prison conditions, a few from mob and militia violence [Braithwaite (1955), pp. 114–15]. Four Quakers were hanged on Boston Common. One of them, Mary Dyer, answered a taunt on her way to the gallows, saying, "Yes, I have been in paradise several days" (see Luke 23:43) [quoted in Braithwaite (1955), p. 515]. Early Friends kept meticulous records of their persecutions. Statistics were periodically presented to the government, in an effort to shame authorities into tolerating these vexing Christian pacifists. But record keeping had a larger sense of purpose. Friends didn't account membership until the 1730s, well after persecutions had ended. Until then, membership in Christ amounted to witnessing and suffering for truth.

But Quaker witness has always ranged between prophetic confrontation and more quiet efforts at persuasion. In the past century the latter has predominated, in a growing variety of forms: training individuals and groups in finding alternatives to violence, lobbying legislative bodies, peace and justice education. But some have always taken the more prophetic path.

For example, before World War I, British Friends worked hard through various channels to avert the conflict. But when war finally broke out, the German threat was so dire and popular opinion was so strong, a third of eligible British Quaker men enlisted. This was by far the largest defection to date from the traditional Quaker refusal of military service. Some, however, took the path of prophetic resistance, despite popular vilification and state abuse. For example, Henry Hodgkin co-founded the Fellowship of Reconciliation, an ecumenical Christian pacifist organization. In doing so, he faced hostile mobs and government surveillance. Some young Friends, such as Corder Catchpool and Wilfred Littleboy, refused any compliance with military conscription and suffered harsh treatment and hard labor in British prisons. Catchpool testified at his trial in 1917:

> I believe there is a heroism other than that which involves the inflic-tion of pain and death: a surer protection for those I love than the slaughter of those whom someone else loves. With God's help I will make the great adventure of faith, standing fearless, unweaponed save with the power of redemptive love [quoted by Phillips in Dandelion, et al. (2004), p. 75].

Later that same year, while in prison, he reflected further on his choice of non-compliance:

> The refusal of early Christians to offer one single grain of incense to a pagan god was, I think, somewhat parallel with our difficulty in admit-ting the slightest measure of compliance with the Conscription Act. I am not sure that Christ's agony in Gethsemane was not essentially a struggle to refuse 'alternative service' to Calvary [again, Dandelion, et. al. (2004), p. 75].

Owing to the resolute strength of their witness, Catchpool and Littleboy became important leaders among British Friends in the next decades.

A more contemporary example of prophetic witness is that of the American Friend Tom Fox, who participated in the Christian Peacemaker Teams (CPT) in Baghdad during the Iraq War. CPT was formed by members of the three Historic Peace Churches (Mennonites, Church of the Brethren, and Friends), although it reaches out to the wider Church as well. CPT places teams of trained peacemakers in war zones and other centers of conflict, to listen to combatants and to those caught in the cross-fire. In 2005, Tom Fox and three other CPT members in Baghdad were kidnapped by an insurgent group and held for several weeks. Fox's murdered body was found in December, around the time the other three were released.

Tom Fox had written a number of personal reflections while work-ing in Baghdad. One written the day before his abduction asks, "Why are we here?" The ensuing answer is to "take part in the creation of the Peaceable Realm of God" in spite of everything. It is to demonstrate *agape,* a "profound respect for all human beings simply for the fact that they are all God's children." He defines "profound respect" as "never thinking or doing anything that would dehumanize one of my fellow human beings." He finds dehumanization as the dominant form of relationship all around him. US forces seek to hunt down and kill "terrorists." As a result of that dehumanizing word, they are killing not only "terrorists" but innocent men, women and children. He concludes that "the first step down the road to violence is taken when I dehumanize a person." Thus, "we are here to root out all aspects of dehumanization that exist within us. We are here to stand with those being dehumanized" [e-mail message from CPTnet, December 2, 2005].

In an earlier, October 2004 reflection, Fox considers the examples of Gandhi and Jesus. He utilizes Walter Wink's translation of Jesus' admonition in Matthew 5:39: "Stand firm against evil." He defines his role in Iraq as standing firm between "the overt aggression of the army" and the "subversive aggression of the terrorist." "But how do you stand firm against a car-bomber or a kidnapper?" He concludes,

> I am to stand firm against the kidnapper as I am to stand firm against the soldier. Does that mean I walk in to a raging battle to confront the soldiers? Does that mean I walk the streets of Baghdad with a sign saying "American for the Taking?" No on both counts. But if Jesus and Gandhi are right, then I am asked to risk my life, and if I lose it to be as forgiving as they were when murdered by the forces of Satan [e-mail message from CPTnet, November 30, 2005].

Guided Conversation

Our experiences with civil authority may be positive or negative. Such authority is necessary to human society (at least as we know it). But it is not always equitable and just. What follows is a meditation on authority. When the demands of civil authority conflict with your sense of Christ's authority in your life, how do you respond? This meditation is not intended to be negative toward authority as such. Rather, it is an exercise in discernment, regarding some area where you experience a conflict of authorities in your life.

As with all the meditations in this book, it is important to take time to be quiet. Find a quiet place to sit for twenty to thirty minutes or more. Sit in a comfortable but upright position. Still your body for a few moments. Feel yourself breathing; perhaps notice the pulse somewhere in your body. As you come to a place of quiet, calm awareness say, "Here I am."

Now bring to mind one of the civil jurisdictions where you live. It may be government at the national, state, or local level. Don't think of it abstractly, but feel yourself physically within its territorial realm. Take a moment to encounter its presence as it bears upon your life. How do you feel toward it—threatened? angry? safe? sad? thankful? Take a moment to savor your relationship to that authority.

Now consider a particular matter where you disagree with that authority's policy. There may be several such matters. Choose one that particularly disturbs you. What's the issue here? What moral or political principle does that authority's action violate? How does that impinge upon your life? What would you like to say to that authority about it? How would you "speak truth to power"? Take a moment to form your thoughts.

If that exercise has agitated you, take a moment to quiet yourself again.

Now ask yourself, where is Christ in this matter? How does Christ embody the important truth you feel has been abridged or degraded by civil authority? Take a moment to feel Christ present with you here and now.

Ask Christ, what is the truth of this matter? What would you have me say? What would you have me do? How can I be your witness in this civil realm? Wait for something to come.

You may find yourself cycling around in your own thoughts and feelings. What comes may feel simply reactive toward civil authority. But wait to feel peace and quiet arise again in you. That is Christ's peace, which may not "answer" your questions any more than Jesus always answered Pilate's. But something may come that you recognize as Christ's Word. It may take the form of prophetic challenge to authority. Or it may be a word of acquiescence. It may lead you toward direct resistance to authority. Or it may inspire you to more patient words of persuasion. It will not be a leading to do violence to anyone.

As you finish this meditation, you might thank Christ for being with you, whether you have felt the Presence or not. If you feel Christ has guided you in some way, pray for courage and patience to follow. May you remain at peace with Christ, whatever words or actions are required of you.

Mary Magdalene
John 20:11–18

Mary Magdalene is depicted in all four New Testament gospels as first, or among the first, to encounter Jesus risen from the dead. She is also mentioned as one who stayed with Jesus at the cross. Only Luke mentions her earlier, as one of the women disciples of Jesus (Luke 8:2). He mentions (as does Mark in 16:9) that Jesus had driven seven demons from her. Her home village of Magdala was only seven miles from Capernaum in Galilee, so she may have been among the earliest followers of Jesus. Although she has been identified over the centuries as a prostitute or as the woman who anointed Jesus at Bethany, no New Testament evidence supports these assertions. We can only conclude that if Jesus liberated her from "seven demons," she must have been healed of some dire condition(s).

Given these scant clues, there is ample room to believe that Mary had a more significant relationship with Jesus than the gospels record. One needs neither a feminist theological agenda nor a romantic imagination to consider the possibility. Feminist New Testament scholars have rightly emphasized the significant encounters between Jesus and the Samaritan woman (in John), the Canaanite (or Syro-Phoenician) woman (in the Synoptics) and Mary Magdalene. These stories suggest that Jesus engaged seriously with women, and that they responded more insightfully than many men, including the "official" disciples of record. Whether Mary was actively pushed out of the earliest Church leadership and largely effaced from the gospels remains a matter of conjecture. Perhaps she faded from the movement for other reasons.

But her pre-eminence among those who first encountered the risen Lord was too significant to be forgotten. It would seem to suggest a particular significance to their relationship and some extraordinary receptivity on her part. It is plausible to suggest that Mary's feminine sensibility allowed her to perceive things in Jesus the male disciples missed. Moreover, if she indeed suffered serious personal difficulties before becoming a disciple of Jesus, those experiences may have enabled her to encounter Christ in an utterly new way, and convey that new awareness to others. Such factors are well attested among some saints, artists, and others in history. The same woundedness might also account for her subsequent marginalization in the earliest Christian movement.

Among the four canonical gospels, John's story of the resurrection singles out Mary for the most dramatic and touching first encounter with the risen Lord. John has told us that Mary was among those who stood near the cross (19:25). In contrast to the other gospels, John has Mary coming to the tomb alone. No other women are mentioned. However, in her report of the empty tomb to Peter and the beloved disciple, she states, "we do not know where they have laid him" (20:2). Perhaps John has chosen to clear the stage for a more dramatic encounter between Mary and Jesus.

In any case, Mary arrives at the tomb while it is still dark, and finds the stone removed from the tomb. She runs to Simon Peter "and the other disciple, the one whom Jesus loved" (John?). She tells them of the empty tomb and conjectures that some unspecified "they" have taken the body somewhere. The two disciples run as fast as possible to the tomb, with Mary not far behind (or who knows? Maybe ahead!). Apparently, the presence or the arrangement of the linen wrappings in the empty tomb causes the beloved disciple to believe that Jesus has been raised. (Perhaps he simply reasons that thieves would not have unwrapped the body before taking it. But in John's gospel, a conjecture would not constitute faith.) In any case, he does not communicate his belief. He and Peter simply return home. Our conversation begins here.

> **20:11–18:** But Mary stood weeping outside the tomb. As she wept, she bent over to look into the tomb; and she saw two angels in white sitting where the body of Jesus had been lying, one at the head and the other at the feet. They said to her, "Woman, why are you weeping?" She said to them, "They have taken away my Lord, and I do not know where they have laid him." When she had said this, she turned around and saw Jesus standing there, but she did not know that it was Jesus. Jesus said to her, "Woman, why are you weeping? Whom are you looking for?" Supposing him to be the gardener, she said to him, "Sir, if you

have carried him away, tell me where you have laid him, and I will take him away." Jesus said to her, "Mary!" She turned and said to him in Hebrew, "Rabbouni!" (which means Teacher). Jesus said to her, "Do not hold on to me, because I have not yet ascended to the Father. But go to my brothers and say to them, "I am ascending to my Father and your Father, to my God and your God." Mary Magdalene went and announced to the disciples, "I have seen the Lord"; and she told them that he had said these things to her.

Simon Peter and the beloved disciple have hurried home to ponder this strange turn of events. (They may also be concerned for their safety as identifiable disciples of Jesus.) But Mary remains at the tomb, weeping. She stands at an abyss of double negation. First, she had watched her beloved die a horrible death. Now even his tortured body is missing. She has lost even that. But she cannot help looking again. This time she sees two angels sitting where the body of Jesus had been. These two mysterious figures in white, positioned where Jesus' head and feet had been, act as reference points to what has been lost. They are after-images of a crucified Messiah. Yet, they are also the beginning of something new. My "red-letter" edition of the New Revised Standard Version Bible prints their words in red. Indeed, this is Christ already speaking to Mary, but beyond her comprehension. Their words come in the form of a question. They still bespeak the negative space of an empty tomb. Their question, "Why are you weeping?" invites Mary to give voice to her grief and confusion. That is foundational to the new revelation about to come. Just as the Israelites groaned in Egyptian bondage before God responded to liberate them, Mary must give voice not only in weeping but in words before she can rediscover her Lord.

Indeed, having articulated her utter desolation, she instinctively turns away from the empty tomb. She turns to see Jesus, but is not yet able to recognize him. Is it the tears in her eyes? Is it the pre-dawn darkness? Is it the ancient, obligatory aversion of a woman's eyes from a strange man? Is it some transformation in the appearance of Jesus? Whatever the case, Jesus repeats the question she has just answered. But he adds, "Whom are you looking for?" The question obliquely intimates not the "what" of a corpse but the "whom" of a living person. It draws her on toward revelation. Misconceiving him to be the gardener, Mary thinks perhaps this man has done something with the body.

Despite the outrage of that supposed action, Mary poses her request carefully, with the deference required toward the "man in charge."

Finally, Jesus calls Mary by name. Now she turns fully toward him, answering, "Rabouni," which is actually Aramaic, not Hebrew. And more than "Teacher," it is "*my* Teacher." Whatever decorum she feels obliged to maintain toward a gardener isn't necessary with Jesus. Whether or not she actually embraces Jesus before his warning, embrace has evidently not been unknown between them. The words "Do not hold on to me" are surely wrenching to Mary in this revelatory moment. But Jesus must continue his movement of return to the Father. Raymond Brown (1970, pp. 1013–14) suggests that in the Gospel of John, the resurrection is just one part of the overall return to the Father. It begins with Jesus "lifted up" on the cross, and ends with his passage into heaven. Only then can he return with the Spirit, as he promised (John 14:3, 16–18). In John, that occurs the evening of the same day, when Jesus comes to the disciples, confirms Mary's good news, and breathes his Spirit upon them.

So the revelation to Mary is the hinge event by which the departure of Jesus will become his return by his Spirit. And as she has turned twice to see and then recognize her beloved teacher, so now she must *turn again* from embracing him, to go and tell the disciples. Mary's unique gift is to recognize the unimaginable and to proclaim the unspeakable. That gift, borne of a deep passage through desolation, makes her "the apostle to the apostles," as some have called her. The message Jesus gives her to declare to the disciples proclaims a new community among them, a familial relation among brothers, sons of the living God. In John 15, Jesus had used the more inclusive category of friendship. Here, Mary is sent to proclaim a message that seems to exclude her as a woman.

In John, we gain the impression of Mary Magdalene as someone very close to Jesus, the person pivotal to the good news of the resurrection, yet not part of the movement's future. Whether she was forced out of the inner circle after Jesus' death, or she dropped out for other reasons is impossible to know. Later writings suggest a clash between Mary and Peter. That may be, although second-century writers may simply have utilized New Testament characters as puppets to dramatize and protest the consolidation of power in the Church by those claiming to inherit Peter's authority. Such later writings also suggest that Jesus gave Mary special revelations that he did not share with the other disciples. That too may be, but such speculation partakes of a gnostic fascination with secret knowledge and insider codes of communication.

Perhaps Mary simply *heard* things in the teachings of Jesus the others did not. Mary may have perceived a deeper, more troubling, but transformative message. Others were simply not ready to hear those overtones during Jesus' lifetime. Her lingering at the empty tomb suggests a willingness to abide in the place of impasse and eclipse. The *via negativa* passage through darkness often receives the most powerful revelations. The beloved disciple began to believe as he looked into the empty tomb. But the breakthrough revelation is Mary's, because she *lingered* there. Such deeper knowledge is not restricted to a select few. But only some will linger long enough in confusion and pain to receive it. (Similar "insider" knowledge comes in Mark 4 to the few who simply tarried long enough to hear Jesus explain his parable of the sower and soils.)

There is an echo in this story of the original calling of the disciples (see Brown, 1970, p. 1010). Jesus asks Mary "Whom are you looking for?" as he had asked the two disciples of the Baptist, "What are you looking for?" (1:38). The disciples respond by addressing him simply as "Rabbi." But as that conversation progresses, they use increasingly exalted titles for him. Here, Mary begins by addressing Jesus as "Rabouni." But when she reaches the disciples, she announces, "I have seen the Lord," the most exalted title, which comes in John only with resurrection and return to the Father. Thus, in following the command to turn and go to the disciples, and then in articulating this amazing news to them, Mary's faith moves from clinging to her beloved teacher to proclaiming the risen Lord.

This story also contains strong echoes of the Song of Solomon 3:1–4 (again, see Brown 1970, p. 1010), which I quote here:

> Upon my bed at night I sought him whom my soul loves;
> I sought him, but found him not;
> I called him, but he gave no answer.
> "I will rise now and go about the city, in the streets and in the squares;
> I will seek him whom my soul loves."
> I sought him, but found him not.
> The sentinels found me, as they went about in the city.

"Have you seen him whom my soul loves?"
Scarcely had I passed them, when I found him whom my soul loves.
I held him, and would not let him go until I brought him into my
    mother's house,
and into the chamber of her that conceived me.

Similarly, a disturbed night likely led Mary to go to the tomb while it is still dark. The angels serve as sentinels in the empty tomb, who likewise offer no answer to her query. But immediately after, she encounters her beloved. She embraces and holds him. In this case, however, Jesus tells Mary to forbear and go tell the disciples the good news. At first, the command seems to break the romantic or mystical union testified in the Song of Solomon. Yet, it is *precisely* in letting go of Jesus and going to bear witness to the disciples that she brings Christ to her inner chamber. She is empowered to preach the good news of "the Lord," and not just "my teacher." The mysticism of the Gospel of John is not about blissful, endless merging with the great "I Am," but a Spirit-filled, Spirit-driven life of witness and service.

In their turn, the disciples will be sent, as Jesus was sent and as Mary has been sent to them. The outward radiation of this revelation will quickly redefine the gospel story, henceforth leaving Mary behind, or at least unmentioned. It is possible that Mary Magdalene participated in early Christian developments but was simply neglected by the New Testament writers. It is also possible that the mission to preach the gospel to the ends of the earth was simply not her calling. In any case, she remains the hinge-character of John's drama. She lingers as a sign to all who mourn in desolation. Her sign offers hints to every great rediscovery of Christ in history. It emboldens those who speak the unspeakable in Christ.

Reflections from the Quaker Tradition

The early Quaker movement was a gathering primarily of Seekers, men and women who could no longer believe or participate in a Christian faith mediated by outward sacramental rites, creeds, formal prayers, etc. As Seekers, they were not happy wanderers. They grieved for the faith and Church participation that had once offered them comfort and guidance. They ached for a fresh, inwardly revealed religion of experience. Writing in 1649, Joseph Salmon compares Seekers to Mary, weeping at an empty tomb. They know only what they have lost. As one of them, he waits to see what Christ's new appearance shall be: "I must stand at the Sepulchre till the voyce be uttered behind me, which I beleeve will be shortly, both to me and to many others" [reprinted in Smith (1983), p. 191]. Salmon was one of the transitional figures between Seekers and Quakers. Like Mary, he faded from view as the new movement took form [for more on Joseph Salmon, see Gwyn (2000) pp. 171–84].

Sarah Jones is another transitional figure, still more shadowy than Salmon. We know very little about her. Possibly the widow of a dyer in Bristol, Jones published a short epistle in 1650, titled *This is Light's Appearance in the Truth*. She doesn't refer to Mary Magdalene at the tomb, but she writes of that sense of desolation. She writes particularly to those who began to receive great revelations but now feel lost, bereft. She begins,

> Dear Lambs, whom the Father hath visited with his eternal love, this is the Message of the Lord unto you, from that word which shall endure for ever, that ye sink down to that eternal word, and rest there, and not in any manifestations, that proceeds from the word. . . . Dear babes, not that the manifestation from the Spirit of truth is denied, for whatsoever is manifested or revealed to the Creature, it is to lead it to the substance, and so that soul and spirit that sinks down into it, it works and levens into its own creature, and it will work out the nature which is contrary to divine nature.

This counsel is similar to what we heard from Isaac Penington in 1661, when he advised Seekers to "sink down to the seed" (see Conversation 8). Jones continues,

> And so, you dear babes, that are little and weak in your own eyes, to you is this message sent, look not at your own weakness, but look at him who is calling you in his eternal love, who will make the weak strong, and will pull down the mighty from their seat. . . . But this is the council of the Lord . . . stand still and see the salvation of God, which is the light of his Covenant. . . . So cease thy mourning, thou weeping babe, that mourns in secret for manifestations from thy beloved as thou hast had in dayes past; for I can testifie unto thee by experience, whosoever thou art in that state, that he is bringing thee nearer him, for that was

but milk which he fed thee with whilst thou was weak, but he will feed thee with the Word from whence that milk proceedeth, if thou be willing and obedient to live at home with Jacob, which is daily to retire thy mind; though the gadding, hunting Esau persecutes thee for it, thou shalt receive the blessing in which all happiness and felicity doth consist for evermore.

This counsel is similar to Fox's advice to Seekers becoming Quakers in 1652 (see Conversation 2). The Jacob-Esau image is also found in some early Quaker writings. Sarah Blackborow made a similar point in 1658, when she chided Seekers for searching outwardly here and there, instead of coming to the truth within (see Conversation 1). Jones concludes,

Therefore come down, come down to the Word of his patience, which is nigh in your hearts, which if you do, he will keep you in the hour of temptation which shall come to try all upon what foundation they are built; for saith Christ, which is the word of God, My sheep hear my voice, and they follow me [see entire epistle in Garman et. al. (1996), pp. 35–37; for more on Sarah Jones, see Gwyn (2000), pp. 203–210].

Jones writes reassuring counsel, grounded in her own experience. George Fox had also broken through in the latter 1640s and was writing in a similar vein by 1650. Yet, while Fox went on to ignite a powerful new movement by 1652, Sarah Jones disappeared.

Guided Conversation

The following may prove uncomfortable, but is potentially transformative. It's an opportunity to look into the empty tomb. The most powerful revelations often come from that disturbing place. If you find yourself in too much discomfort, stop the meditation. You may wish to discuss the experience with a trusted friend or mentor. On the other hand, perhaps nothing will come of this meditation for you. But its general shape may remind you of a significant past experience, or prepare you to receive a future one.

As with all the meditations in this book, it is important to take time to be quiet. Find a quiet place to sit for twenty to thirty minutes or more. Sit in a comfortable but upright position. Still your body for a few moments.

Feel yourself breathing; perhaps notice the pulse somewhere in your body. As you come to a place of quiet awareness say, "Here I am."

Briefly consider something causing you anxiety, pain or sorrow at this time in your life. Perhaps something that makes you feel lonely, lost, inadequate, ashamed. Don't immerse yourself in it. Just witness it afresh.

Now, set that matter aside and see what lies behind it. Not an explanation or a cause. At a deeper level, what lies behind the matter? Not simply more things that trouble you. Set those aside too. Behind all that, what's there? As you sit with that question, you may confront a deeper sense of dread, something not tied to circumstance. If you find it, stay there with it a while. If it's too troubling, of course you may simply end the meditation. Or, if you can't get beyond the circumstantial issues in your life right now, you might try this meditation again at another time.

If you are able to continue, don't be alarmed. You are simply confronting the abyss that's at the center of each of us. Yes, you are the hollow person you always suspected yourself to be! But coming to that emptiness is much more useful than worrying about it. Like Mary, now you are now alone in a desolate place. Weep for yourself, if you are moved to weep. Or have a good laugh at yourself, if that feels right. Otherwise, simply stay quietly there at the abyss. It may become a place of great stillness and beauty.

Now, consider this question: "Whom do you seek?" "Who is the beloved your soul longs for here?" Ponder the question a moment. There are individuals in your life whose company and comfort you would welcome right now. But they are not the answer. They can't really be here with you right now. Wait here very quietly.

You may sense something shift. It may seem oblique or peripheral to your focus of attention. Turn your attention toward it. Who or what is there? Stay with the encounter while you can. Let it unfold. Neither grasp at it nor run from it. After it has faded, remain a moment longer in the peace, refreshment and joy of the encounter.

During or after this mediation, you may feel led toward some future action. It may be something specific, or just a more general sense of direction. Try to absorb it, to understand what's been given you. If you feel uncertain about it, you could check this leading with someone you trust.

But if this meditation produces nothing for you, don't be dismayed. At the empty tomb, nothing is nothing. Christ abides with you somewhere in that negative space. Sitting quietly with the emptiness may be your portion this time. It's our portion most of the time. Learning to abide peacefully with Christ, even when his presence feels like absence, is the fullest expression of your friendship. But if you're feeling really desperate, don't hesitate to seek the help of someone you trust. You can come back and sit quietly with Christ another time.

Simon Peter

John 21:15–25

The final conversation with Simon Peter sustains the poignancy of the preceding one with Mary Magdalene. As Mary has been turned from devastating grief to become "apostle to the apostles," first to bear the good news, now Simon Peter will be rehabilitated from despair over his denials of Jesus the night of the arrest, to become first among the apostles. In both cases, "the disciple whom Jesus loved," presumably John, figures prominently. Yet, John witnesses ungrudgingly to the prime roles of both Mary and Peter. If there was indeed a conflict between Mary and Peter (there definitely was a conflict between their champions in later generations), John is interposed between them as a mediating voice.

Following the appearance to Mary at the tomb and two encounters with the disciples, the Gospel of John seems to conclude with the final verses of Chapter 20. Chapter 21 appears to be a second ending appended to the original. But it offers important closure on Peter's failure. It establishes him as the central figure in the beginnings of the Church, not by virtue of his earlier intimacy with Jesus, nor through the sheer force of his personality, but on the basis of Christ's call.

The scene finds Peter and the disciples returned to Galilee—by no means busy founding a new movement. Rather, they are at the Sea of Tiberias (as the Sea of Galilee was better known to Greek-speakers). John has never mentioned that Peter and Andrew were fishermen from this area. This may be another detail he assumes we know from other sources. In John 16:32, Jesus had predicted that they would be scattered at his death. Despite the stunning revelations of their risen Lord in Jerusalem, they have not yet taken up his work. Perhaps it is because their most catalytic member, Peter, is still adrift. When he announces one evening that he's going fishing, the others readily answer, "We will go with you." We can imagine they are anxious to support him. Might they even fear that he is suicidal?

But an entire night of fishing produces no results. In the morning, as they draw near the shore, Jesus calls to them from land. But again they do not recognize him immediately. His advice to recast the nets recalls Luke's story. In both versions, the successful catch prefigures the future mission of the Church, even if John's Jesus doesn't explicitly promise that they will someday "catch men" (Luke 5:10). The specific number of fish caught, 153, has been subject to wide-ranging interpretations over the centuries. Whatever the specific symbolism may be, it seems to suggest some kind of completeness or perfection, a world-embracing scope for Christian mission.

The risen Christ treats the disciples to breakfast on the shore. By now, they all know who is speaking to them, yet they cannot bring themselves to acknowledge it. They are still tongue-tied apostles. The breakthrough comes with Peter. And so, in front of the group, Jesus begins his conversation with Peter.

> **21:15–19:** When they had finished breakfast, Jesus said to Simon Peter, "Simon, son of John, do you love me more than these?" He said to him, "Yes, Lord; you know that I love you." Jesus said to him, "Feed my lambs." A second time he said to him, "Simon son of John, do you love me?" He said to him, "Yes, Lord, you know that I love you." Jesus said to him, "Tend my sheep." He said to him the third time, "Simon, son of John, do you love me?" Peter felt hurt because he said to him the third time, "Do you love me?" And he said to him, "Lord, you know everything; you know that I love you." Jesus said to him, "Feed my sheep. Very truly, I tell you, when you were younger, you used to fasten your own belt and go wherever you wished. But when you grow old, you will stretch out your hands, and someone else will fasten a belt around you and take you where you do not wish to go." (He said this to indicate the kind of death by which he would glorify God.) After this he said to him, "Follow me."

Jesus addresses Peter rather formally: "Simon, son of John." Jesus must reach out to Peter with a solemnity that matches his crushing sense of failure and guilt. Belittling that terrible fact will not help. So Jesus' three questions—and Peter's three pained protestations of love—will walk him back through his three denials and break their numbing grip on him. In John 13, Peter had confidently asserted his loyalty to Jesus, even to the death. This time, he appeals to Christ's own knowledge of his heart, that he loves him. But each time, Jesus asks Peter to *express his love by tending and feeding his sheep*. This is not a closed circle of mystical union with the divine. It is love poured out through service to others, just as the Son did not remain in cozy exaltation with the Father but became flesh, lived, taught, and suffered among us. This is Peter's opportunity, not to redeem himself but to *live out* his redemption in servant fellowship with his Lord. Peter's triple commission establishes him as shepherd among shepherds, apostle among apostles. It is a powerful covenantal moment: it both cuts him loose from his past and binds him to a radically new future (recall the paradoxical meaning of the Hebrew word for covenant, *berith*, which means both to *cut* and to *bind*).

There has long been debate over the Greek words translated "love" in this passage. In his first two questions, Jesus uses the verb *agapein* to ask if Peter loves him. Both times, Peter responds affirmatively, but substitutes the Greek *philein*. *Philein* often connotes mutual friendship, while *agapein* often suggests a love that prefers one over all others, even oneself. Hence, the first time, Jesus asks, "do you love me more than these?" (that is, more than these closest friends). Finally, in the third question, Jesus shifts to *philein*, and Peter confirms with *philein*. What's going on here? Is Peter simply unable to rise to a higher love, *agapein*, and Jesus has to "settle" for *philein*? Some have understood it so. But as Raymond Brown finally summarizes (1970, p. 1103), there is no conclusive evidence to establish such an interpretation. There is no consistent difference in usage between *philein* and *agapein* in John's gospel overall. Still, John surely suggests something with this sequence. It is possible that Jesus' use of *agapein* the first two times is to remind Peter of his brave promises before Jesus' arrest and his denials. Peter responds with *philein*, earnestly hoping to regain the friendship Jesus had described in his conversation about the vine and branches. When both of them finally use *philein*, perhaps it suggests that true friendship has been restored. In any case, John clearly uses this story to confirm Peter's primacy among apostles.

Jesus moves directly on from his third commissioning to predict Peter's martyrdom (returning to the overtones of sacrificial love implied by *agapein*?). Interestingly, the imagery here could simply imply that Peter will grow old and have to be bound and carried around on a litter. But John makes it explicit that Jesus prophesies Peter's eventual martyrdom (tradition has it that Peter too was crucified.) Jesus concludes, saying simply, "Follow me." The call ironically echoes and overturns one more detail from the night Jesus was arrested. Peter had then protested, "Lord, why can I not follow you now? I will lay down my life for you" (John 13:37). Now Jesus invites him to do just that.

> **21:20–23:** Peter turned and saw the disciple whom Jesus loved following them; he was the one who had reclined next to Jesus at the supper and had said, "Lord, who is it that is going to betray you?" When Peter saw him, he said to Jesus, "Lord, what about him? Jesus said to him, "If it is my will that he remain until I come, what is that to you? Follow me!" So the rumor spread in the community that this disciple would not die. Yet Jesus did not say to him that he would not die, but, "If it is my will that he remain until I come what is that to you?"

The invitation to follow Jesus is apparently effective immediately. Peter and Jesus are walking together when Peter turns and notices the beloved disciple following behind them. This is the most perceptive of the disciples, due to his intimacy with Jesus. He was first to believe Jesus had been raised (even before seeing the risen Lord). He was first to recognize Jesus standing on the shore in this scene. And, with more echoes of the night Jesus was arrested, John reminds us that the beloved disciple had responded most directly to Jesus' announcement of betrayal. Having been confronted with his own future martyrdom, Peter wants to know that disciple's destiny. This verse seems to imply some jealousy or rivalry between Peter and the beloved disciple. Jesus implies a different destiny for the latter, but chides Peter that it is none of his concern. Jesus repeats, "Follow me," in order to turn Peter from comparisons and rivalry. Jesus is the pattern that matters. Peter and the beloved disciple will each have a distinctive genius of discipleship and role to play in the beginnings of the Church.

> **21:24–25:** This is the disciple who is testifying to these things and has written them, and we know that his testimony is true. But there are also many other things that Jesus did; if every one of them were written down, I suppose that the world itself could not contain the books that would be written.

The second ending to the gospel identifies the beloved disciple with the writer of the Gospel (identified by tradition as John). It is probably

John's community that confirms, "We know that his testimony is true." *How* do they know? It's unlikely that they are all eye-witnesses to the life and teachings of Jesus, so they cannot confirm a *literal* truth in John's testimony. And, although there is much *literary* quality to John's stories, would that establish them as *true*? Perhaps the community verifies the truth of John's testimony because the conversations formalized in this Gospel are grounded *in the community's own lived conversation with Christ.*

Such an interpretation would make sense of the apparent hyperbole that follows. An unidentified editorial "I" supposes that the world would not contain all the books that could be written about everything Jesus did. Perhaps the editor alludes to the widening conversation with Christ during the first decades of the Church. Like the first disciples, everyone thereafter who engages in that conversation could add more to what Jesus has said and done. The conversation transcends history. It bridges time and eternity. The conversations of the earthly Jesus and the conversation of the risen Lord down to this day are all one expanding conversation. Likewise, the mystery of Christ's true identity continues to unfold as we continue to find our identity in Christ.

We noted near the beginning of Conversation 4 that in John's usage, "the world" tends not to refer to the physical universe but the realm of human knowledge and activity carried on in alienation from God's light, truth, and love (see also Conversation 2). All the misunderstandings of Jesus in John's gospel are by men and women whose consciousness is distorted by the world's categories. By contrast, John's Prologue affirms that the physical universe, "all things," was created through the living Word (John 1:3). So, if the editor is speaking of "the world" in the same sense we find elsewhere in John, then indeed *nothing* Jesus has said and done, and nothing that is truly testified of him, could be contained by it. The world cannot receive the Spirit of truth, "because it neither sees him nor knows him" (John 14:17). But "Be of good cheer, for I have overcome the world" (John 16:33 KJV).

Reflections from the Quaker Tradition

In Quaker history, no leader has fallen as devastatingly or been restored as powerfully as James Nayler. In Conversation 6, we noted the provocative sign of Christ's coming that Nayler and a few followers enacted in the streets of Bristol in 1656. We also mentioned Parliament's elaborate show-trial and savage punishment of Nayler as a false Christ.

Nayler's story is complicated by his alienation from the other Quaker leadership at the time of the Bristol incident. A small group of admirers had drawn Nayler aside and encouraged him to resent the leadership of George Fox and the main body of Friends. After his trial and punishment by Parliament, Nayler languished in prison and his sympathizers openly harassed Quaker meetings, especially around London. Their actions added to the growing popular backlash against the movement. Meanwhile, some of Nayler's oldest and closest Friends from the north, in particular William Dewsbury and Richard Hubberthorne, sat quietly with him (like the disciples with Peter) and gently worked to recover him.

Eventually, in two written statements, Nayler repented of his betrayal of the movement and disavowed his envious followers who had "made use of my name" in attacking Friends. (He never repented of his symbolic action in Bristol, which Fox himself affirmed as a valid sign.) Nayler gave thanks for his true friends, who "came to me in that time in true pity, and in sorrow of heart suffered with me for all that was befallen me, and that precious truth I had [formerly] walked in." In describing the manner of his own defection, he also warned others to recognize the spirit of envy toward God's people:

> By this shall you all perceive that spirit whatever it pretends, it will secretly withdraw your entire love from the flock of God already gathered, and cool your affections and zeal toward their present meetings, and if you judge it not there, it will grow on with an evil eye, to spy out their failings, and delight to hear of them, and talk of them with a hidden joy whispering them to others and adding thereunto, with a desire to see them broken . . . until it be seated in the throne of open enmity and strife against the lambs of Christ, preferring the society of the profane before them, and taking part therewith against them, joining with any who seek to scatter them . . . and so they in whom this is entered, being exalted above the living witness in themselves, would devour it in others.

This is a probing analysis of the canker of resentment, by one who had fallen deeply under its spell, but who eventually found his way back to humility and love in Christ. Nayler's betrayal was different from

Peter's case of stark panic and denial. But like Peter's recovery, Nayler's return was painful and difficult. He warns,

> All of you, in whom any measure of this precious life hath been betrayed, either through this or any other thing, that to the light thereof you may return in yourselves, and there wait till the life arise, which is your return, and which must give you rest with the flock of God, for it's the life that's the door and the fold, and without it you will be but wanderers, and lost in all your thoughts and motions. . . . Therefore in the bowels of tender love I warn you all, to take heed how you ever come under that spirit under any pretense whatsoever; but let the fear of God and sound judgment in the spirit of meekness preserve you all above it; for wheresoever it enters by consent, it is hardly got out again; and if it be, it is not without much sorrow; and this I have found in the depth, which I declare in plainness and truth, as I have learned from the Lord.

Apart from the flock, where group discernment can keep one honest and humble, the individual easily becomes a law unto his or her own self, a solipsistic wanderer.

Nayler's health was broken by the time he was released from prison in latter 1659. He returned to effective ministry among Friends around London for a few months. In June 1660, he started on his way home to Yorkshire, but was robbed and severely beaten on the road by unknown assailants. He died of his injuries a couple days later. The following words are often credited as his dying words. Although they were actually written earlier, they beautifully articulate the Christ-like bearing Nayler gained at the end of his journey.

> There is a Spirit that I feel that delights to do no Evil, nor to revenge any Wrong, but delights to endure all things, in Hope to enjoy its own in the end; its hope is to out-live all Wrath, and Contention, and to weary out all Exaltation and Cruelty, or whatsoever is of a Nature contrary to itself, it sees to the end of all Temptations, as it bears no evil in its self, so it conceives none in thoughts to any other, For its ground and spring is the Mercies and forgiveness of God; its Crown is Meekness, its Life is Everlasting Love unfeigned, and takes its Kingdom with Intreaty, and not with Contention, and keeps it by lowliness of mind; in God alone can it rejoyce, though none else regard it, nor can own its life. Its conceived in Sorrow, and brought forth without any to pitty

it, nor doth it murmur at Grief and Oppression; it never rejoyceth but through Sufferings, for with the Worlds Joy it is murthered; I found it alone being forsaken, I have fellowship therein, with them who lived in Dens, and desolate Places in the Earth, who through Death obtained this Resurrection, and Eternal Holy Life [For more on Nayler, see Bittle (1986) and Gwyn (1995), Chapter 5].

Guided Conversation

The following is an opportunity to experience forgiveness and restoration in Christ, in the pattern described in this chapter's conversation. It is an opportunity to lay to rest and move on from some careless, selfish, or uncourageous act you regret, something that may be holding you back from a fuller life in Christ. As with all the meditations in this book, this one may not meet you where you are just now. Even if it does, perhaps not all its features will be helpful to you. Just see if the overall flow of the meditation is useful to you at this time. If not, it may prove helpful some other time.

As with all the meditations in this book, it is important to take time to be quiet. Find a quiet place to sit for twenty to thirty minutes or more. Sit in a comfortable but upright position. Still your body for a few moments. Feel yourself breathing; perhaps notice the pulse somewhere in your body. As you come to a place of quiet, calm awareness say, "Here I am."

As you come more fully into your body, take a moment to recognize Christ there with you. Christ abides there with that sense of wholeness, aliveness, peace. Come to rest there with Christ in your body. Let Christ refresh your spirit for a few moments.

Now take a moment to consider some past incident when you feel you didn't act or respond well. The memory may bring an uncomfortable pang of conscience, perhaps even a physical sensation. Even if you have done all you can to atone with others for your mistake, it may still bother you. Rather than turn away from it, take a moment to witness that feeling. Don't entangle yourself in it. Stay at the edge of it, but with sustained attention.

What word or phrase describes the feeling? Or is there an image it conjures in your mind? Take a moment to identify, name that quality. Sit with that name or image for a few moments, to sense whether it is right. If it doesn't seem right, find something that fits better.

Now, ask yourself, is my love for Christ—this sense of goodness, wholeness, and peace—greater than that? If you can answer "yes," what is Christ asking you to do? Take a moment to receive any leading that comes.

Again, ask yourself, is my love for Christ closer to me than that? If you can answer "yes," what is Christ asking you to do? Take a moment to receive any leading that comes.

Once more, ask yourself, is my love for Christ able to outlive that? If you can answer "yes," what is Christ asking you to do? Take a moment to receive any leading that comes.

The sense of leading may remain consistent all three times, or it may change and develop. Perhaps you are led to do something further to repair a damaged relationship. Or you may simply feel more able to move on. This meditation does not mean to suggest that your love for Christ simply outweighs any sense of guilt or regret. Rather, it returns you to the deepest reality, and from there you can experience forgiveness more fully and live out your redemption in fresh and creative ways.

If you found you were unable to answer "yes" at least by the third time, you might return to the centering in Christ that began this meditation. But if you are experiencing trouble, stop and try this meditation another day.

CONCLUSION

'Before Abraham Was, I Am'

Much as I love the Gospel of John, I have sometimes felt irritated by its portrayal of Jesus as omniscient. For example, when Jesus sees a hungry crowd coming his way, he asks Philip where they will buy bread to feed so many people. The narrator hastens to add that Jesus "said this to test him, for he himself knew what he was going to do" (6:6). Worse, those who oppose Jesus seem almost destined to do so. Jesus seems to scorn them, rather than appeal to them.

I'm glad we have the other three New Testament gospels alongside John. They give Jesus a more human countenance. They offer us a more human drama, in which people make choices for or against Jesus. Perhaps John knew these other gospels (or at least the traditions that were eventually finalized in those documents) and assumed hearers/readers would also. For example, we noted in Conversation 11 that John doesn't explain who Pilate was. He seems to assume that we know him from other sources. John is more concerned to elaborate the trial of Jesus before Pilate in order to reveal the dynamics of Christ's truth *versus* political power. So perhaps the Fourth Gospel was always intended to stand alongside other traditions about Jesus, each telling the story from a different perspective.

But what *is* John's perspective? Among other things, there is a strongly *ex post facto* quality. The story is told so rigorously from the perspective of Jesus' death and resurrection that nearly all sense of human drama is effaced. In law, an *ex post facto* statute is enacted in response to a precipitating event but made effective retroactively. Similarly, the ultimate destiny of Jesus bears strongly upon every event in John's story. This effect is jarring to our modern sensibilities. But perhaps John simply offers the same perspective on the *time* of Jesus that we noticed in his perspective on the *identity* of Jesus. In conversation after conversation, we have heard people misunderstand his true identity and intention. While they focus on physical substances or worldly circumstances, Jesus uses those things to draw their attention to another level. When Jesus states that "I am" the "true" or "living" water, bread, light, or gate, he draws our attention from things in time to himself in the eternal.

The true identity of Jesus as the living Word keeps exploding our categories. Nowhere is this more scandalously stated than at the conclusion of John 8. That conversation with "the Jews" is the most conflictive and alienating in the entire Gospel of John. Countryman (1994: p. 46) classifies it among the "obnoxious discourses" in John. Jesus' claims are so extravagant that his hearers are almost stampeded into positions for or against him. Here, Jesus attacks his hearers' self-identification as descendants of Abraham. They identify themselves with Abraham by means of a commonsense *time-line* of ethnic derivation. They are thinking in linear terms. By contrast, Jesus claims to be the Son of the Father (the Eternal). He further claims that Abraham, a man of true faith, had insight into Jesus' coming into the world, and rejoiced in it. His hearers sarcastically ask when Jesus, less than fifty years old, saw their ancient ancestor rejoicing. Jesus hurls back one more outrageous claim: "Very truly, I tell you, before Abraham was, I am" (8:58). That is, Jesus claims pre-existence and pre-eminence in relation to Abraham. In so doing, he rends the very fabric of time. This is an *apocalyptic* moment, a rupture in time, a tearing of the veil that masks the true, eternal nature of things. His hearers can bear no more; they pick up stones to hurl back at Jesus. This exchange offers us clues to John's strange treatment of events in time.

For John, the life of Christ *comprehends all time*. To enter into these conversations is to feed upon Christ's flesh and blood, to drink his living water, to rise to the understanding, love, and obedience of life in Christ. To enter into these conversations is to *in-habit the Gospel*. Of course, I refer not to the book or the words as such, but to the overall constellation of conversations that comprise life in Christ. As we enter into these conversations more deeply, we are still in the world, but not of it. We are still in time, but not of it. The meditations at the end of each chapter of this book provide practice in grounding our awareness of Christ in our bodies, of the eternal in our time.

In Greek, John's Prologue states the incarnation with a syntactical ambiguity that implies a dynamic tension between Christ's unique incarnation in Jesus of Nazareth and Christ's incarnation in each person. The New Revised Standard Version of the Bible offers two possible translations of verse 9: "The true light, which enlightens everyone, was coming into the world"; or "He was the true light that enlightens everyone coming into the world." These two renderings offer different emphases while stating a single truth. That is, the Word became flesh and became the light of the world in the person of Jesus, in order to help us know and follow the same Word becoming flesh in our bodies and enlightening our lives. The Word in Jesus and the Word in us enter into conversation through our deepening devotion, faithful community, and service to our fellow humans. There is no time between the time of Jesus and our time. There is no time but this present, eternal moment.

To state the matter differently, the raising of Jesus is not simply what happens next, after his death and burial. John reports the raising of Jesus as an event in time. But we know its truth only as Christ *raises us* to the eternal perspective. As Jesus says to Nicodemus, "just as Moses lifted up the serpent in the wilderness, so must the Son of Man be lifted up, that whoever believes in him may have eternal life" (3:15). Heaven is wherever, eternity is whenever, we grow in conversation with Christ.

In his first published tract, *To All That Would Know the Way to the Kingdom* (1653), George Fox writes,

> The first step of peace is to stand still in the light (which discovers things contrary to it) for power and strength to stand against that nature which the light discovers: here grace grows, here is God alone glorified and exalted, and the unknown truth, unknown to the world, made manifest, which draws up that which lies in the prison, and refresheth it in time, up to God, out of time, through time [Fox (1831) 4:17–18].

Fox's triple prepositions—in, out, and through time—evoke the subtle interaction of eternity and time in Christ. One by no means flies away from the world, with its troubles and opportunities to bask in God's love. But one does live by a truth the world does not know and cannot contain.

Twenty years later, persecutions continued to ravage the Quaker movement. In 1671, Fox suffered a serious illness, induced partly by the spiritual oppression he felt on behalf of his suffering friends. During his illness, he had a vision of the new Jerusalem, as described by John in the Book of Revelation (Chapter 21):

> And whilst I was in my travails and sufferings I saw the state of the city New Jerusalem, which comes out of heaven . . . which the professors had looked upon to be like an outward city or some town that had come out of the elements. . . . The spiritual reign of Christ Jesus in this great city . . . is within the light, the city of the living God. . . . so here is the city within the light [where] there is no place or language, but there his voice may be heard. The gate stands open night and day that all may come in here. . . . I am just in the city. . . . This true city is come down since the apostles days and is coming down from God. . . . All that are within the light of Christ and his faith . . . and within the Spirit . . . come to this heavenly city, New Jerusalem [quoted in Gwyn (1986), p. 199–200].

Here we find an other-worldly image from the Bible grounded in this world's reality. To live in the light is to live within the city, where there is no delimited place, time, or language, but where the voice of Christ is heard and followed, in the concrete circumstances of our lives.

And so, we continue our journeys in, through, and out of time. Along the way, periodic rereading of the Gospel of John brings fresh insight and encouragement, because we revisit those conversations at new stages in our own conversation with Christ. Christ abides below the intellect, and deeper than the deepest feelings. But from there, Christ raises both heart and mind to new life. And in these bodies, Christ renews our daily faithfulness to God and neighbor.

Works Cited

Ambler, Rex. *Truth of the Heart: An Anthology of George Fox*. London: Quaker Books, 2001.

Ambler, Rex. *Light to Live By*. London: Quaker Books, 2002.

Anderson, Paul N. *The Christology of the Fourth Gospel: Its Unity and Disunity in the Light of John 6*. Valley Forge: Trinity International, 1997.

Bittle, William G. *James Nayler, 1618–1660: The Quaker Indicted by Parliament*. Richmond, IN: Friends United Press, 1986.

Braithwaite, W. C. *The Beginnings of Quakerism*, second edition. Cambridge: Cambridge University Press, 1955.

Braithwaite, W. C. *The Second Period of Quakerism*, second edition. Cambridge: Cambridge University Press, 1955.

Britain Yearly Meeting. *Quaker Faith & Practice*. London: Britain Yearly Meeting of the Religious Society of Friends, 1995.

Brown, Raymond E. *The Gospel of John*, vol. 1 (Anchor Bible Commentary). New York: Doubleday, 1966.

Brown, Raymond E. *The Gospel of John*, vol. 2 (Anchor Bible Commentary). New York: Doubleday, 1970.

Countryman, William. *The Mystical Way and the Fourth Gospel: Crossing Over to God*. Valley Forge: Trinity International, 1994.

Dandelion, Pink, Gwyn, Douglas, Muers, Rachel, Phillips, Brian, and Sturm, Richard E. *Towards Tragedy/Reclaiming Hope: Literature, Theology, and Sociology in Conversation*. Burlington, VT: Ashgate, 2004.

Fox, George. *Works*, 8 vols. Philadelphia: Gould, 1831.

Fox, George. *Journal*, John L. Nickalls, ed. Cambridge: Cambridge University Press, 1952.

Garman, Mary, Applegate, Judith, Benefiel, Margaret, and Meredith, Dortha, eds. *Hidden in Plain Sight: Quaker Women's Writings, 1650–1700*. Wallingford, PA: Pendle Hill, 1996.

Gendlin, Eugene T. *Focusing*. New York: Bantam, 1981.

Gwyn, Douglas. *Apocalypse of the Word: The Life and Message of George Fox*. Richmond, IN: Friends United Press, 1986.

Gwyn, Douglas. *The Covenant Crucified: Quakers and the Rise of Capitalism*. Wallingford, PA: Pendle Hill, 1995.

Gwyn, Douglas. *Seekers Found: Atonement in Early Quaker Experience*. Wallingford, PA: Pendle Hill, 2000.

Heller, Mike, ed. *The Tendering Presence: Essays on John Woolman*. Wallingford, PA: Pendle Hill, 2003.

Kelly, Thomas. *The Eternal Promise*. Richmond, IN: Friends United Press, 1977.

Martyn, J. Louis. *History and Theology of the Fourth Gospel*. Nashville, TN: Abingdon, 1979.

Mather, Eleanor Price. *Edward Hicks, Primitive Quaker: His Religion in Relation to His Art*. Pendle Hill Pamphlet #170, Wallingford, PA: Pendle Hill, 1970.

Penington, Isaac. *Works*, vol. 2. Glenside, PA: Quaker Heritage Press, 1994.

Penington, Isaac. *Works*, vol. 1. Glenside, PA: Quaker Heritage Press, 1995.

Penington, Mary. *Experiences in the Life of Mary Penington (Written by Herself)*. London: Friends Historical Society, 1992.

Rensberger, David. *The Johannine Faith and Liberating Community*. Philadelphia: Westminster, 1988.

Smith, Nigel, ed. *A Collection of Ranter Writings from the 17th Century*. London: Junction, 1983.

Whitmire, Catherine. *Plain Living*. Notre Dame, IN: Sorin, 2001.

Wink, Walter. *The Human Being: Jesus and the Enigma of the Son of the Man*. Philadelphia: Fortress, 2002.

Woolman, John. *The Journal and Major Essays*, Phillips P. Moulton, ed. Oxford: Oxford University Press, 1971.